OUT OF MY MIND

OUT OF MY MIND

An Autobiography

Kristin Nelson Tinker

Harry N. Abrams, Inc., Publishers

Editor: Terry Hackford
Designer: Martine Bruel

Portions of the text and some illustrative materials in this book are reprinted by special permission.
See pages 228-230 for all credit information. Every effort has been made to credit sources of text and
illustrations correctly. If any credits have been inadvertently omitted, please contact the publisher.

Library of Congress Cataloging-in-Publication Data

Tinker, Kristin Nelson, 1945-
Out of my mind : an autobiography / by Kristin Nelson Tinker.
p.   cm.
ISBN 0-8109-3691-7
1. Tinker, Kristin Nelson, 1945-   .   2. Painters — United States — Biography.
3. Tinker, Kristin Nelson, 1945-   — Notebooks, sketchbooks, etc.   I. Title.
ND237.T557A2   1997a
759.13 — dc21   97-7730
[B]

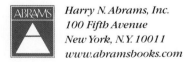

Harry N. Abrams, Inc.
100 Fifth Avenue
New York, N.Y. 10011
www.abramsbooks.com

For Tracy, Matthew, Gunnar, and Sam

Contents

Acknowledgments

Grateful acknowledgments are made to the following:

For their enthusiasm, talent, and generosity of spirit, I wish to thank my editor, Terry Reece Hackford, and my art director, Martine Bruel.

My friends: Jane Hallaren, for her love and unfailing sense of humor, keen insight and discerning eye, John Longenecker for his patience, kind heart, and invaluable assistance, and Gastone Rossilli, for his enduring friendship, love, and for coming to the rescue one more time.

Jim McMullan, Joanna Mondragon, Wynel Cary, Wally Franson, Paula Mason, Susan Tyler, Tisha Sterling, Ann Sothern, Tim Harmon, Martha Burke, Joanna Preyer, Lisa Knox Burns, Roberta Knox, Doug Dutton, Anthony Cuñha, Cynthia Wick, Dr. Tim Burke, and Tony Scully.

James Watson Webb, Jr., Carol Weinstock, Alice Jay, Peter Ackroyd, and Roberta Scimone, who offered wisdom and encouragement.

Gratitude, appreciation, and deep respect to Eric Himmel at Harry N. Abrams, Inc., and my agent, Ed Breslin, who rode in like the calvary and saved the day.

The friends and relatives who shared family history with me and helped to fill in the missing pieces—especially to my mother—who was never sure if this book was a good idea—for her courage and compassion.

My four children whose loving support means everything.

My granddaughter, Remi, who blesses my life.

And special thanks and all my love to my husband, Mark, who among many other things, knows how to spell.

MIRACLE

1987

1996

When I was approached about doing a book of my paintings, I thought it would take six months to pull all of the work together. I'd kept a photographic record of the paintings throughout the years with the dates of their completion and a list of collectors. How difficult could it be? A half dozen incarnations and five years later, I realize my estimate was a little optimistic.

Because each of the paintings has a source of inspiration—a memory, poem, song lyric, special correspondence, a personal protest or statement, a hope or dream—my original idea was to present each work with a small amount of background. But what started out as a relatively uncomplicated concept quickly became an intricate journey, for in order to describe each painting, I had to undertake a soul-searching and sometimes painful recollection of the experience that lay behind it. I came to realize, however, that as much as I feared going back to the past, coming to terms with it sustained me.

I chose to write the book in journal form. Parts of the text are taken from actual journals that I kept and from poems that I wrote at the time. Other entries are written from and filtered through memory.

For many years, my identity was as an appendage of two families. One was my birth family and one was the family into which I married. Both families were the personification of the American Dream.

My father, Tom Harmon, was a national sports hero before the days of mass media and instant replay. My mother, Elyse Knox, was a cover girl and movie actress who gave up her career to raise three children. I am the eldest, born Sharon Kristin on June 25, 1945, at the end of World War II. My sister, Kelly Jean, was born in November of 1948 and my brother, Thomas Mark, in the fall of 1951. We were a family of competition, achievement, and celebrity.

Growing up, I was frustrated by an inability to be heard or have my feelings validated. In my family, honest communication was extremely difficult and keeping a record of feelings, especially if they were remotely unpleasant, could have consequences.

Most of the time, I lived in my own world. I had a self-willed system of withdrawing and a private place in the storage space built into the top of the closet in my bedroom, where I made families out of cardboard, fabric, and paint. I thought about someday having a big room where I'd be able to create and make a mess—as it was called—undisturbed.

The books in my father's library and television were my frame of reference. I dreamed of one day marrying Ricky Nelson, who would rescue me and take me away. By the time I was seventeen, Rick and I had been dating steadily for two years and I was a high-school graduate making wedding plans. When I was young, dreams had a way of coming true.

Ozzie and Harriet Nelson became my in-laws. For many years, I wanted to

1

be just like them, until I began to understand the complexity of this family who were role models to a nation.

After my marriage to Rick, I'd fill in the blanks on forms and job applications depending on how I was feeling that month. At various times in the sixties, I wrote: "Student," "Housewife," "Actress," "Dancer," "Mother." "Homemaker" was substituted for "Housewife" in the seventies when "Producer" and "Agent" were added and interchanged. In the eighties, I wrote "Casting Assistant," "Casting Director," and checked the "Divorced" box for the first time.

The thing is, I've always been a painter. But in thirty-three years, ever since my first painting at seventeen, whether I was working on a commission or painting for a one-woman show, I'd never once written "Artist" in the blank.

The early eighties were spent mourning the loss of a dream and blaming everyone else for my misfortune. I wasted large amounts of time abusing drugs and alcohol, lost in self-pity and the great black spaces that accompanied the end of my marriage. In that dark place, I had great excuses for not taking my paintings seriously and spent time flying on borrowed celebrity wings.

1987 was a year of extremes and a turning point for me. It brought the best and worst life could offer. That spring, I suffered a breakdown and hospitalization. I went through rehabilitation and was sued for custody of my youngest son by my brother.

That summer, I met my future husband, Mark Tinker. My daughter was married, diagnosed with Hodgkin's lymphoma in the fall, and began her long road to recovery at Christmas. It was also a year of liberation when I realized that I had nothing left to lose, and in doing so, found I was able to proceed with courage.

As I brought the paintings and text together for this book, I could see the essence of my life emerging through the paintings as well as the paintings emerging from my life. The paintings are stories of the lessons I learned— lessons of self-worth and self-loathing, joy and sorrow, depression, addiction, recovery, well-being and acceptance. My story is still incomplete, but this is where the past and present have reconciled.

This book began as an effort to document the paintings, but because life and art are inseparable, it's the story of a life as well. It's taken a long time to call myself an artist.

Kristin Nelson Tinker

Los Angeles, California

PEPPERTREE

1994

CHAPTER ONE

1962–1969

"OUR HOUSE"

In my journal

March, 1962

I've recorded private details that have been finding their way into family conversations. Obviously, someone's reading my stuff. It isn't safe to write anything down in this house.

A letter to me from a boy at Stanford had "opened by mistake—sorry" written across the ripped envelope in my mother's careful penmanship.

April, 1962

I found a hole in the back of the pedestal sink in my bathroom—a secret place for my diary. Now I can write what I want. No one will ever find my diary there.

May, 1962

What an optimist—what a dope. Why would I think I could keep my diary a secret? Someone's been in it again— it was replaced upside down. It's the most awful feeling. They're a bunch of spies—all of them—pretending to be innocent when I ask them about it. My privacy means nothing and my feelings are just fodder for family gossip.

Bubbles La Tour,
Burr Head,
and Moody McGillacuddy,
1958

My little sister and brother and I compete for my parents' attention. Everything's based on appearance—it's how we look, not how we feel, that's most important. Kelly and Mark are quiet, happy, and obedient. It seems like I'm always grounded. I was the only one that my father ever spanked. My brother said it made him jealous.

My father nicknamed all of us. He calls my mother "Butch," my grandmother "Cupcake" or "General," my sister "Bubbles La Tour," my brother "Burr Head." I'm "Moody McGillacuddy."

My mother says to stop being so dramatic and tells me to look on the bright side.

May, 1962

Rick is the only person I can really talk to. He's very shy, but we understand each other. He's a wonderful and sensitive listener and I try to be the same for him. I'm so lucky that he loves me.

June, 1962

His name is Rick (Eric Hilliard) Nelson. It's hard to describe just how handsome he is. He'll be twenty-three next May. He has dark blue eyes, dark thick hair, long lashes, the most beautiful face. He doesn't act like he's famous—he's completely unassuming, quiet, and very reserved. We can talk about anything. Sometimes we don't have to talk at all.

I paid close attention watching him grow up on TV. I was ten in 1956 and remember when my mother came back from seeing this new guy, Elvis, in Las Vegas. And she talked about his "sexy swivel." I may have been young, but I wasn't swayed. Elvis was old and greasy, and my dreams were set on Rick.

I felt we were meant to be together someday . . . that it was just a matter of time.

Rick and I met when I was twelve. He was playing in a basketball game against my father's team. I asked for his autograph and had my picture taken with him. He didn't ask me out for another three years. He later admitted he was scared of my father.

On our first date, we had dinner at his parents' house. The Nelsons were very nice. We ate in their dining room and liver was served. I hate liver and I found it difficult to smile and carry on a conversation while holding my breath. But I made it through the meal.

June, 1962

Graduation Day. Twelve years of Catholicism and table etiquette are OVER! No more hypocrisy! No more rules!

The absolute best of all was that, for graduation, Rick gave me a "pre-engagement" ring—a pink pearl surrounded by tiny diamonds. I'm the luckiest girl on the planet.

September, 1962

He talks about getting married. I haven't mentioned anything to my parents, because my father wants me to go to college.

I would love to be his wife more than anything. We've discussed announcing our engagement at Christmas and getting married in the spring.

I'm the luckiest girl on the planet.

October, 1962

I'm not used to adults paying attention to me. His parents actually listen and look at me when I'm speaking to them. They're considerate of my feelings and interested in what I have to say. They treat me as if I matter.

November, 1962

I love the ballet. I've been dancing since I was four years old. When I was eleven, I danced the Sugar Plum Fairy on a Christmas TV special and Rick's mother, whom I'd never met, wrote me a fan letter. I remember she wrote that "all her fellas" sat in front of the TV to watch me perform.

In all these years since, I've thought about Rick watching me dance. I go back over every step, picturing him in front of that television . . . and wonder what he must have been thinking when I did this pirouette . . . and this jeté . . .

. . . and now I'm going to be his wife —a part of his family.

November, 1962

The Nelsons have a large collection of primitive paintings at their home in Hollywood. They're by a midwesterner named Streeter Blair, an antiques dealer by trade, not an artist. The Nelsons tell me he's never been schooled in art at all. He doesn't know about perspective—mixing colors—the basics —he just paints, unintimidated and free of restriction. All this is a new concept for me—to paint by instinct— strictly from the heart.

I study these paintings. I know I could never paint like my mother . . . but I now see there is more than one way to paint, and a way in which there's no "wrong" or "right" involved.

Just paint! No rules, no limits!
A way to keep a secret record...

November, 1962

In the bathroom—painting in secret behind the sliding doors of the bathtub. No one looks for me here—no one looks over my shoulder.

The idea is a painting of the whole family on the front lawn at Christmas . . . a farewell gift for my parents because this will be my last Christmas at home.

November, 1962

I wonder if everyone identifies numbers and letters by color the way I always have.

For example: R is deep red, I is white, C is yellow-orange, K is pink. The colors of the letters and numbers are specific and clear in my mind and they don't vary. I haven't been able to translate the colors I see onto paper, but I'll keep trying.

December, 1962

The painting is almost finished. As far as I know, it's still a secret. I'm sewing a Christmas tree skirt for Rick's brother and sister-in-law and a mantel cover for his parents, too.

December, 1962

Rick and I drove to Laguna yesterday to pick out an engagement ring from the little jewelry store. We found a ring almost exactly like his mother's . . . a yellow gold band and an antique diamond in a Tiffany setting. It's perfect.

Christmas Eve, 1962

At the Nelsons' Christmas Eve party, after the buffet dinner, we announced our engagement. Our families and friends toasted with champagne. It was a very special night—we decided to get married on the twentieth of April, my grandparents' anniversary.

Christmas Day, 1962

Rick arrived around noon to be with me when I gave Mom and Dad the painting. They were completely surprised. My mother wanted to know who the artist was.

The nicest gift this Christmas was that I realized I'd found a way to keep a secret record of times, thoughts, events, feelings—not by writing in a diary, but by painting my memories and feelings within the images on the canvas.

April 19, 1963
Tomorrow's the big day!
I'm floating through a haze of activity in a house full of visiting relatives and friends.
We're going to be married at St. Martin's in Brentwood
and have our reception in the backyard of our house.
Nana made waffles with white syrup this morning for breakfast.
The smell of frying bacon and hot coffee coming up the stairs
sent waves of nausea through me again.
I'd like to tell everyone that we're expecting, but no one knows except us.
Propriety is everything to our families.

April 20, 1963
Just said good-bye to the folks . . . again . . . They drove down to the airport
to surprise us and see us off after the reception . . . Waiting . . . good-bye again . . .
again good-bye good-bye . . .

. . . the great escape's begun.

GLORY TRAIN
1963

April 20, 1963
Wedding notes on
the red-eye to New York

It was a fairy-tale wedding—
my dream come true.

The bridesmaids and I
were made up by the makeup
man from Rick's show (who
insisted I wear lipstick). My
sister, unsmiling in her new
braces, was maid of honor
and my little brother was
an altar boy. Rick's brother,
Dave, was best man. (All the
Nelson men looked like they
hadn't been to sleep.)

The press waited for us
outside the church and took
a lot of pictures.

It was windy and cold at
the reception; the guests wore
coats while waiting in the
reception line. My mouth
ached from smiling so much.
(Rick said that when I walked
down the aisle, all he could
see was a big red mouth.)

My handsome prince came
and took me away.

When we left for our
happily ever after, rain began
to fall.

I was heavy with mascara
and awe.

April, 1963 Paradise Island, The Bahamas
One more week and this island—my father's "Oh-you-can-see-Europe-anytime" recommendation
—closes for the season.

There's hardly anyone here—there's nothing to do.
I don't play golf and won't play tennis with Rick because he was nationally ranked in the "fifteen-and-unders."
He's way out of my league.

I sit on the beach, wrapped in a towel,
drawing hermit crabs, and try not to be sick.

A-bomb tests in the Pacific are the reason there's no sun.

I cried last night because Rick squashed a bug on the wall of our room.
I imagined the bug going home to her babies and escalated the story in my mind
until I just couldn't stop crying.
It seems silly now.

I'm not hungry by the time room service arrives.
When Rick comes in, he scrapes off my plate so the waiter "won't think he's killed me or something."

I'm homesick.

I've never been this far away from home.

May, 1963
Nassau to New York to LA
Ever since we drove away from the reception and I looked at him sitting next to me,
I've had this thought that runs around and around in my head and keeps repeating: "NOW WHAT?"

May, 1963

Mom said she'd meet us in LA, but she was late—so we took a cab home.

Picture a little love nest
Down where the roses swing
Picture that same sweet love nest
Think what a year can bring

She's so ambitious, it even shows
She's washing dishes and baby clothes
So don't forget folks
That's what you get folks
For makin' whoopie
   Gus Kahn / Walter Donaldson

June, 1963

Wonder what being newly married would be like under normal circumstances. These are heady times as Mrs. Nelson. Rick's father genuflects when he sees me. I know Catholics make him nervous and he's trying to be funny, but it's embarrassing.

July, 1963

We told our families that we're expecting in October. Our parents were very happy, but when Rick told them exactly when the baby was due, his father smiled that smile of his, rocked back and forth on his heels, and mumbled, "Oh, great . . . great . . . great . . ."

But behind his back he was counting the months on his fingers.

I worked on the Nelson show for the first time. The crew was called in from their hiatus to film the show that introduces me as Rick's wife. The storyline wouldn't work if I were brought in any more pregnant, so his father decided to shoot the show early.

I like acting. His dad is patient with me and the crew is great. Working together for so many years, they made me feel right at home. At this moment, I can honestly say that my head and stomach are equally swelled.

October 25, 1963

After eighteen hours of labor, our daughter was born at St. John's Hospital in Santa Monica. She's so beautiful. All eyes and perfect.

Goodnight, my angel
Now it's time to dream
And dream how wonderful your life
  will be
Someday your child may cry
And if you sing this lullabye
Then in your heart
There will always be a part of me

Someday we'll all be gone
But lullabyes go on and on
They never die
That's how you
And I
Will be
     Billy Joel

October, 1963

We named our baby Tracy Kristine. I won't be able to touch her or hold her for five days—until we take her home. For appearance' sake, our daughter's been placed in an incubator. The Nelsons have announced her birth as "premature." It makes my baby unreal to me.

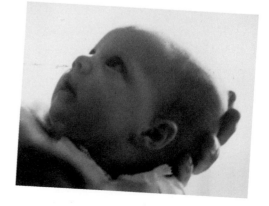

November, 1963

The dream is to be perfect

"WHEN THE KENNEDYS WERE IN THE WHITE HOUSE"

KRISTIN NELSON

November, 1963

President Kennedy was shot at noon in a motorcade in Dallas. He died at 12:31 P.M. on the way to Parkland Hospital. This is a bad dream.

My beautiful daughter
asleep and well
what kind of world
are you born into?

They buried the president today. They moved his personal things out of the White House as the new administration moved in. His desk . . . his rocking chair. A profound sadness overwhelms me. How old everyone seems.

December, 1963

I miss his youth
spirit
passion
vulnerability
his elegant and courageous wife.
his little children

There are no words
> *despair*
>> *emptiness*
>>> *futility*

A great dark place in my heart

Our generation had so much hope that we could make a difference . . .

December, 1964

I've been working on a painting for Mrs. Kennedy for almost a year.
It's the only way I know to tell her I'm sorry.

January, 1965

I didn't send her the painting.
I don't know how to paint.
I doubt I ever will.
> *What is it that I do exactly?*

June, 1966

My father calls me an "old married lady." I was twenty-one yesterday and my parents threw a surprise party down in the playroom of the Carmelina house. They invited mostly family and a few friends.

I really wanted to GO OUT and dance.

July, 1966

My very shy husband said he was going to bring the White House painting to the art dealer who handles Streeter Blair. For him to take the initiative is unbelievable—he's painfully uncomfortable around strangers.

Her name is Sari Heller and she's primarily a Naive—or Primitive—art dealer. I'm sure her enthusiasm was influenced by Rick's bringing the painting in person, but she likes my work! She wants to give me a show and expects "twenty paintings at léast" by next March.

He is a gentle man, my love
   He faces straight the sun
He traces softly on the grass
   gently gets things done
He speaks not in metaphors
   of rising costs and hopeless wars
But only of the land and sea
   and hope and love and loving me
No other on this earth shall be
   This patient one who easily
Takes me through life's painted face
   with goodness and amazing grace.

Twenty paintings is a lot. Tracy's almost three now—taking ballet lessons twice a week before my class and going to nursery school for a few hours every other morning. I get home from dropping her off in time to leave to pick her up—there's never enough time and so much to do. It's hard to find time to paint. It seems so long ago I had any time at all.

December, 1966

Turpentine and barbells . . . I took over a corner of Rick's gym—am trying to keep out of the way.

Dear Kris,

I thank you for making me so happy! I'm so proud to be married to someone like you. Life wouldn't have any meaning to me if I couldn't share it with you.

I thank you for giving me the chance to love you

I Love You Very Much!

Rick xxxxx xxxxxxxxxxxxxx xxx xx x xx x x xxxxxxxxxxxxxxxxxxx xxxxx xxxxx

February, 1967
*S*ome of the paintings come
from dreams—others from
photographs—music—lyrics
—poetry. Some are wishful
thinkings.

We're expecting again at
the end of September.

March, 1967
*A*ll twenty-seven paintings
are hanging in the gallery—
enough paintings to cover
three walls. The preview
reception is tomorrow night,
so I have overnight to come
up with something that'll
cover the last wall.

I'm back in the gym with
one very big canvas and my
father, who volunteered to
help fill in the blades of grass.

STILL WET YET

1967

Death of Kennedy Inspired Girl to Start Art Career

The assassination of President John F. Kennedy did many things to many people.

A teen-age girl from North Hollywood, who had never attended an art class, felt a compulsion to take a brush in her hand and begin dabbing at a piece of canvas.

Using a photo of the White House as her only guide, she began to fashion a scene as it might have been in happier days.

On the lawn a touch football game was in progress. Two children were playing with Robert F. Kennedy. Jacqueline Kennedy was in a horse drawn cart with other youngsters. The President walked toward the cheerful activity.

Planned It as Gift

For a year and a half young Kris Nelson labored on her creation. "I planned to give it to Jackie," she said, "but then I didn't think she would like it."

The young lady, having discovered she is a natural artist, also worked on 21 other paintings.

On Sunday her primitives, as they are called, went on display at the Sari Heller Gallery at 9463 Charleville Blvd., in Beverly Hills. The exhibit will continue throughout the month.

March, 1967

The paintings are on display and people are actually coming to see them. I feel like apologizing.

Today the gallery was closed, but Sari Heller was there to let me in. She was going on about the opening. Last night almost every painting was sold!

Then the phone rang. Senator Robert Kennedy was calling—for me—from New York. Sari was suddenly pale.

She handed me the receiver. "Hello?"

He said that he was calling on behalf of his sister-in-law and that she had seen the invitation to my show, which had a print of the White House painting on the cover. He said Mrs. Kennedy wondered if the painting were still available, because she would like to purchase it.

My heart was racing. I managed to tell him the painting had always been hers— that I had painted it for her. I promised I would ship it as soon as the show closed and thanked him for calling personally. I hung up and thought I was going to pass out.

What an amazing time this is!

United States Senate
WASHINGTON, D.C.

May 9, 1967

Dear Mrs. Nelson,

     I just wanted you to know how much all of us appreciate your painting of the White House. It is a very impressive work.

     I am sorry we did not have a chance to see each other in New York during your last trip. I hope we will see you soon.

     Again, many thanks.

Sincerely,

Robert F. Kennedy

June, 1967

We're expecting TWO babies in September and both sides of the family take credit. Rick's grandmother reminds him that she's a twin and that her mother was a triplet. My father brings over a family tree to prove there are twins on the Harmon side—seven sets in one family, actually.

July, 1967

Sixty-five pounds heavier and two months to go. I have a brace with suspenders to support my stomach, which is very attractive. Rick walks ten feet ahead or ten feet behind when we're in public and he thinks I don't notice.

August, 1967

It's hot. Spending time in the air-conditioned Olds wagon—my face up to the blower—or at the Nelsons' beach house. Rick isn't off the road until the end of September, when the babies are due.

It's impossible to be comfortable or in one position for any length of time. I've been able to manage only a few paintings.

Tracy says she wants to be a mermaid when she grows up. She's requested a sequinned fish tail.

MOM'S LAGUNA

1967

I.

Dear Kris,

Well I just got there doing a show and I'm a little bit tired and sweaty but no more than usual. It's last call for Katy Winters time.

I saw your Aunt and Uncle tonight at the show and I remembered which ones they were, they were Mr. and Mrs. Harmon from Detroit.

I'm sending you a picture and a review of the show and I think its a good one, but I'm not sure. Everyone has been telling me that they've really been carving up all the acts around here so I think I got off easy. As much as I can figure out I'm a clean cut Mod looking Ozzie Nelson with a twang of Ray Charles (after RITTER). Or will at least I cover all the fields. I think I've got to write smaller or something

(or OVER)(OVER) ———

August, 1967

I *try not to think about his life on the road, but I'm reminded of his mother's curious advice before we were married: "NEVER surprise him by showing up on the road."*

This is the time to remember
Cause it will not last forever
These are the days
To hold on to
Cause we won't
Although we'll want to
This is the time
But time is gonna change
You've given me the best of you
But now I need the rest of you
                    Billy Joel

I'm a travelin' man
Made a lot of stops
All over the world
And in every port
I own the heart
Of at least one lovely girl
                    Jerry Fuller

23

II. Jacks leaving in the morning and It's really goina be a drag like I said when I talked to you last night. (I wish I was coming home this week) but I guess it won't be too much longer (11 more days) from now.

Things have been going real good for me here. Like I said their sold out for this whole week and It looks good for next week also.

I hope you feel alright and arn't doing anything foolish like pole vaulting or scuba diving or anything like that, and what ever you do don't sneeze because I'd like to be their when the big events happen.

Well I'd better sign off for now because this letter has taken me a little while to write. So as the big golden sun rises in the West or is it East I'm goina say goodnight, and Give my Love to Tracy and everyone and I hope things are fine at home. OH I almost forgot give Alex a big kiss for me.
(All kidding aside tho) I really miss everyone but most expecially I miss YOU!
All My Love
Rick (P.S. How about Herbert + Herbert)

August, 1967

It seems like an eternity, but it was only six years ago that I begged my parents to take me along to his older brother's wedding:

Rick was divine
David was not

*I wore a pillbox hat
hair in a flip
yellow and white
polka-dot dress
waist cincher
stockings with seams
so he'd notice I was wearing them
and one-and-a-half-inch heels*

*At the reception
He said hello to my parents
and to me
and went home
with the maid of honor*

MAY 20, 1961
DAVE AND JUNE'S
WEDDING

1967

September 20, 1967

This afternoon—at 3:01 and 3:34, respectively—Matthew Gray Nelson and Gunnar Eric Nelson were born at St. Joseph's Hospital in North Hollywood, California—the same hospital where I was born twenty-two years ago.

November, 1967

A recurring dream of my childhood home on Sunswept Drive has come with the two new babies—dreams to explore and paint. They come almost every night as little problem solvers in my sleep.

When my father returned from China at the end of World War II, he built a cozy, brown-shingled house for his family in the foothills of Studio City. Ours was one of the first houses built on the narrow, winding street called Sunswept Drive and my father had the opportunity to pick our address. As with most numbers in my young life, this one included a 98—the number he'd made famous playing football at the University of Michigan.

When my sister was born in 1949, my parents added a bigger bedroom for themselves. Three and a half years later, when my brother Mark came along, Kelly and I moved in together and her room was redone in blue-and-white-check for the new baby. Additional rooms became necessary: a bedroom and bath for my grandmother, who came to live with us after I was born; a room over the garage for Heidi and then Meta, who helped my mother and grandmother with us.

Our house had a living-dining area and a bay window with a view of the San Fernando Valley, my whole world. My father built a kid-size country store in our backyard. We had a peach tree, rose bushes, a boxer dog named "Roger," and an assortment of poodles with variations on the name "Bo."

In my dream, a warm, yellow light floods through Sunswept. I sit in the window, looking at my world through my mother's collection of colored glass. I especially love the rich, red color of the crystal bell. I'm safe in my home with my grandmother close by in her kitchen. She's at the core of my dream, as she was in my life.

December, 1967

My father has asked for a painting of golf—his favorite pastime—for Christmas. I can't think of many things less interesting to me than a golf course. And golf will forever represent something that took him away.

I was having trouble with his painting. Then I remembered the familiar and comforting sound of football on TV on Sunday afternoons. The warm memory of my father watching the game as my mother and grandmother hovered round him allowed the painting to come more easily.

January, 1968

I've always idolized my father. When his playing days were over, he worked as a sportscaster and was on the road with various teams for much of my childhood. I confused him with Hopalong Cassidy. He looked and sounded like Hoppy to me and they were both my heroes. I dreamed of finding Topper parked in the garage.

My father was a remote and powerful presence. I wanted to be his best pal—his trusted confidante. I'd read into his silences the ways I perceived he loved me, trying to understand his Irish ways of affection—through loud words, merciless kidding, and unspoken loyalty.

Fortunately for me, he's a prodigious letter writer. His letters allow for the insights I need to understand him. I've always wanted him to be proud of me—although with passing time, I'm resigned to never being perfect enough for his unqualified approval. And more than anything, I want him to tell me he loves me.

Me and my dad. Ours is a complicated relationship.

PA'S BEL AIR

1967

MAIN STREET THEN

1968

February, 1968 **The dream again**—*the house on Sunswept—*

only it is larger—*two-storied*—*from the past—*

there are people everywhere

*—I don't know them—there are children—*strangers *on the front lawn—*

where is the recipe?—there will be nothing to eat if I don't cook—
A voice from far away—who is the blonde man sitting beside me?—I can't make out who he is.

I want to go back.

As Rick's parents have reminded him since he was little—
my parents remind me now that I have an obligation and responsibility to the public.
How long before I'm discovered?
This pretender with polite manners, firm handshake, and eager smile
who isn't exactly what she seems—
the discontented one who questions still and looks for more?

"The longing comes when one has given scant time to the mystic cookfire or to the dreamtime,
too little time to one's own creative life, one's life work, or one's true loves."

Clarissa Pinkola Estés

My mother says I'm capable of making my marriage anything I want.
But what substitutes for passion?

March, 1968
I was raised to complement a man—to be a stabilizing, problem-solving, nurturing homemaker—
to see to it that my family ran smoothly.
I'm a wife and mother before anything else and I'm doing the best I can,
but domesticity leaves a lot to be desired.
Who's responsible for me not having a room of my own—for not making time to paint?

What was the dream anyway?

29

March, 1968

It looks as if this will be the last year of the Nelson show. The boys are overdue to be out on their own and Harriet wants a rest. Ozzie has decided that in order to keep the show on the air, he will carry the storylines rather than divide them among family members as he's done in the past. And he's decided Rick's public shouldn't see him working with his wife anymore. It's bad for Rick's image. But everyone's all grown up. Rick's no longer the irrepressible Ricky with the flattop and squeaky voice. He's twenty-eight and a father himself. His father should let go.

I've been on the show since 1963. In the past five years, Rick and I have done a few movies together and we've worked separately. I love the idea of bringing a character to life, but I'm ambivalent about acting altogether. I don't like having to depend on someone else in order to work at something I love.

April, 1968

ABC cancelled the show after all. The Adventures of Ozzie and Harriet ran for eighteen years. The first five years were on radio and the last thirteen on television.

May, 1968

I don't ask Rick to help me or encourage him to take over some of the responsibility of the household or part-time care of the children. This is woman's work and I am superwoman. Born and bred to do it all.

But I need time for myself.

They say I have everything. But an intangible emptiness filters through the days.

May, 1968

I have a commission for a painting of an antique shop on the Sunset Strip. I'm trading the painting for an old mantel in the store. It's made of hand-carved pine and stripped of paint— from a turn-of-the-century house in East Los Angeles.

To paint . . . to dance . . . There is peace for me in these places.

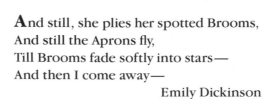

And still, she plies her spotted Brooms,
And still the Aprons fly,
Till Brooms fade softly into stars—
And then I come away—

Emily Dickinson

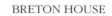

"BRETON HOUSE"
KRISTIN NELSON
2-16-68

June, 1968

Driving down La Cienega Boulevard, there was a FOR RENT sign in the second-story window of an old fourplex, so I stopped to look around.

Upstairs, a long front room was built in tandem with another and there was a small back porch with good light from the large windows.

This had been someone's home once. A fireplace mantel remained to protect an old gas heater. A ventilation pipe was in the ceiling. Wood floors showed through worn carpet and the rent was reasonable. An instant decision was made—this would be my own place—

I have my own studio.

My upstairs rooms are magical for me. The first painting is going quickly—a good sign. I imagined a campaign rally for Senator Robert Kennedy. I've never seen him in person, but I've read all about him and admire him very much. I think he's extremely courageous to be running for president.

"...Standing by himself on the lid of the trunk of his convertible—so alone, so vulnerable, so fragile, you feared he might break. He was thin. He did not chop the air with his hands as his brother Jack had; instead he had a little gesture with his right hand, the fist closed, the thumb sticking up a little, and he would jab with it to make a point. When he got applause, he did not smile at the crowd, pleased; instead he looked down, down at the ground or at his speech, and waited till they had finished, then went on. He could take a bland generality and deliver it with such depth of feeling that it cut like a knife."

John Bartlow Martin

The unthinkable happened. Two days ago, Senator Kennedy was shot in the head after making his victory speech in the California primary. He died this morning. He was only forty-two years old.

AND ASK WHY NOT

1969

The times they are a-changin'

Bob Dylan

July, 1969

Rick's working on a TV special on the streets of San Francisco. Rick's producer, John Boylan, is here, too. John's been an inspiring friend—encouraging both of us to more clearly define our dreams. Since they've been working together, Rick's been writing his own songs and seems so much happier.

There are war protests daily. People wear wreaths of flowers, colored beads, embroidered everything. Holding lighted candles, they pray for the soldiers and sing in the streets.

Did you ever want to go
where you've never been before?
Did you ever want to know
things you've never known before?
I'll take you there with me
and maybe then you'll see
It's easy to be free

Rick Nelson

LOMBARD STREET

1969

PERSPECTIVE

1969

His Countenance—a Billow—
His Fingers, as He passed
Let go a music—as of tunes
Blown tremulous in Glass—

He visited—still flitting—
Then like a timid Man
Again, He tapped—'twas flurriedly—
And I became alone—

Emily Dickinson

Lyrics by
John Boylan

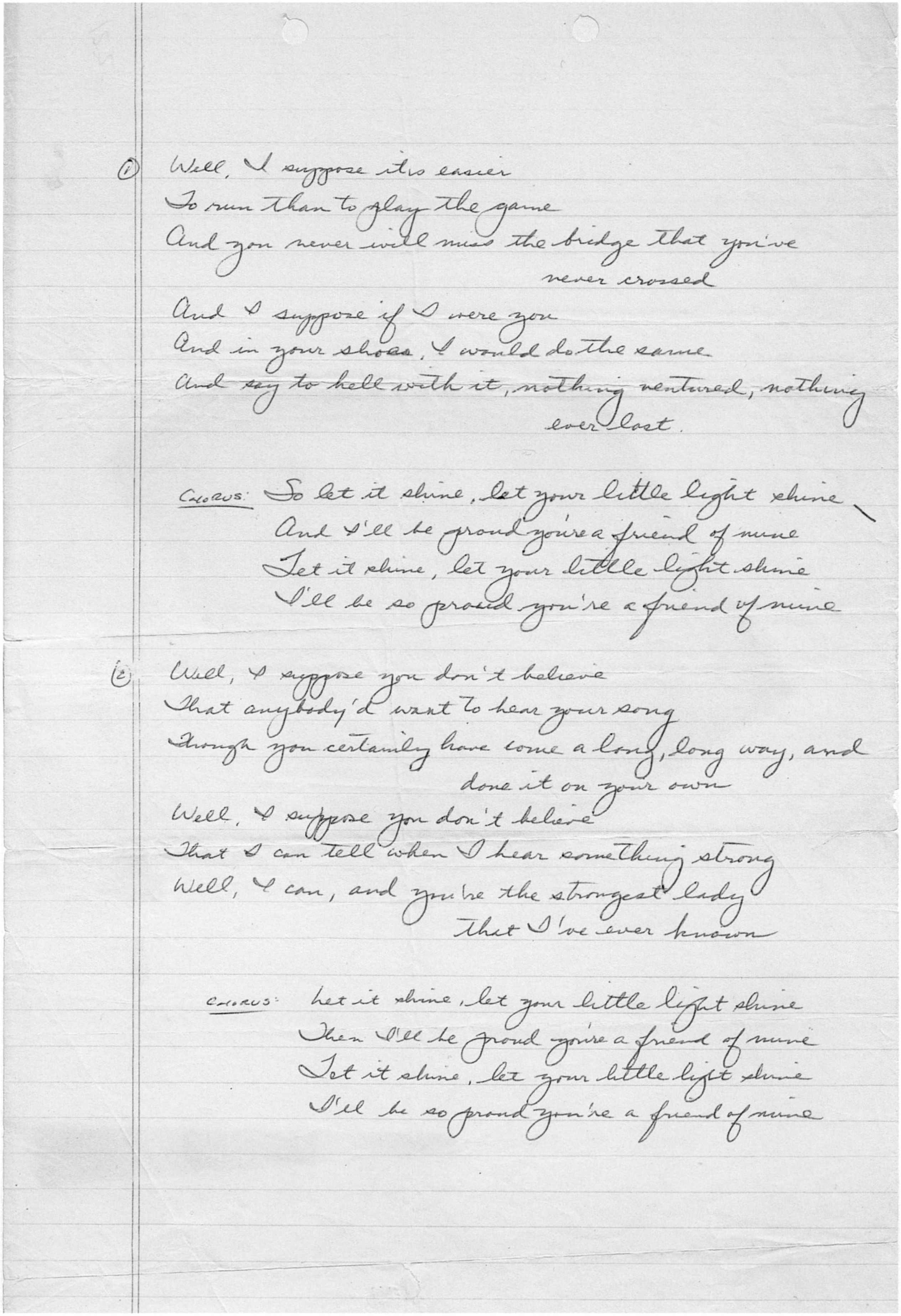

① Well, I suppose it's easier
To run than to play the game
And you never will miss the bridge that you've
never crossed
And I suppose if I were you
And in your shoes, I would do the same
And say to hell with it, nothing ventured, nothing
ever lost.

Chorus: So let it shine, let your little light shine
And I'll be proud you're a friend of mine
Let it shine, let your little light shine
I'll be so proud you're a friend of mine

② Well, I suppose you don't believe
That anybody'd want to hear your song
Though you certainly have come a long, long way, and
done it on your own
Well, I suppose you don't believe
That I can tell when I hear something strong
Well, I can, and you're the strongest lady
That I've ever known

Chorus: Let it shine, let your little light shine
Then I'll be proud you're a friend of mine
Let it shine, let your little light shine
I'll be so proud you're a friend of mine

August, 1969

For my mother and father's silver anniversary, I painted their wedding day using personal recollections and yellowed newspaper accounts from my father's scrapbooks.

On a summer's day in 1944, my father—all-American First Lieutenant Thomas Dudley Harmon of Rensselaer, Indiana—married my mother, actress Elyse Knox of Hartford, Connecticut, in Ann Arbor, Michigan.

My mother had her wedding gown made from the silk parachute that saved my father's life. A newspaper cartoon from that day pictures the happy couple walking out of church as a gust of wind inflates the bride's skirt and carries her away.

Contrary to published reports, my mother did not embroider around the bullet holes.

SILVER LINING

1969

TO MOM AND DAD
ON THEIR TWENTY-FIFTH
WEDDING ANNIVERSARY
AUGUST 26-1969
"THIS PAINTING HAS ITS SILVER LINING"
ALL MY LOVE, KRIS

September, 1969

David Lichine has asked me to re-create
the role he originally choreographed for
Leslie Caron in his ballet "La Creation"
for the premiere performance of the
Ballet Society of Los Angeles.

His wife, Tatiana Riabouchinska
(Tania), has been my teacher since I was
a little girl. Beautiful—spirited—
courageous and kind, she's the most
inspiring woman I know.

It feels wonderful to be in shape
and

dancing again.

"When will someone rescue the human heart that lies inside the ballerina?"
Margot Fonteyn

CHAPTER TWO

1970–1971

If I can stop one Heart from breaking
I shall not live in vain
If I can ease one Life the Aching
Or cool one Pain

Or help one fainting Robin
Unto his Nest again
I shall not live in Vain.

                    Emily Dickinson

GET TOGETHER
1970

...skin colors as they were intended.

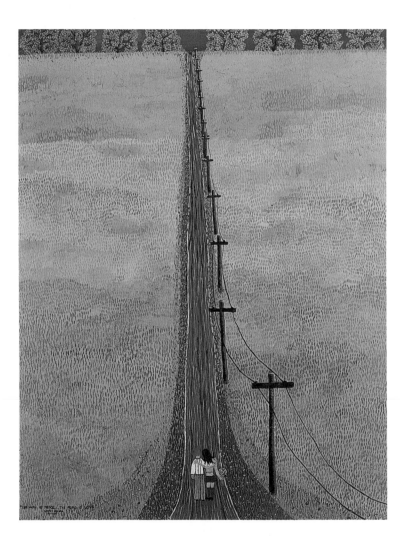

THE WAY IS PEACE/
THE ROAD IS LOVE

1970

February, 1970

A *representative from a national telephone service suggested I come up with some images for a new communications campaign. Two paintings are complete, but they have to be approved before they can be used.*

T*he representative came by the studio today to see the paintings. He approved* The Way Is Peace/The Road Is Love *but* Get Together *caused immediate dissension.*

He: "You'll have to paint all the figures white—the children are every color and they're holding hands—this is unacceptable in the southern states."

Me: "Doesn't everybody use the telephone?"

He: [No response.]

Me: "I won't change the skin colors to match."

He: "Then your painting isn't suitable for our needs."

And with an anemic handshake and uncomfortable good-bye . . . he left. The children will remain in the painting as I intended them to be.

A road is just a road
That the one you love is leaving on
Midnight's another dawn
A hundred miles ago

John Jennings
Mary Chapin Carpenter   *45*

March, 1970
Rain makes everything easier
warming the earth
Inspiring morning
with repetitive drops

soothing
diamonds on the glass
irregular paths
to the woods below

the birds sing a sad song

I'm glad it's raining
alone in a half light
it's almost enough

I hold this moment
wrapped in a blanket
and wish it would storm

April, 1970
Seventh Anniversary

We've changed in seven years,
Rick and I.
He has his music. I have
painting and dancing. We
share three beautiful children
and come together during
the infrequent times he is off
the road. We don't talk about
our differences. It's easier to
remain silent than to speak
of growing apart. We don't
talk about separate lives
or our independence from
each other.

Overnight, very
Whitely, discreetly,
Very quietly

Our toes, our noses
Take hold on the loam,
Acquire the air.

Nobody sees us,
Stops us, betrays us;
The small grains make room.

Soft fists insist on
Heaving the needles,
The leafy bedding.

Even the paving.
Our hammers, our rams,
earless and eyeless,

Perfectly voiceless,
Widen the crannies,
Shoulder through holes. We

Diet on water,
On crumbs of shadow,
Bland-mannered, asking

Little or nothing.
So many of us!
So many of us!

We are shelves, we are
Tables, we are meek,
We are edible,

Nudgers and shovers
In spite of ourselves.
Our kind multiplies:

We shall by morning
Inherit the earth.
Our foot's in the door.

Sylvia Plath

america
Winner is Everybody
YOUTHS
RAMPAGE
PEACE IN
SIGHT
Space Program Benefits
HAMBURGER
EARTH DAY
All Ages Join Pollution War
In Celebration of Earth Day
DUKE
BIG WINNER

April, 1970

I am full of words, paintings, colors.

A parade of people forms every night just after the sun goes down on the Sunset Strip.
They gather in front of the Whiskey, celebrating peacefully and joyfully—
a life-affirming army of feathers, beads, and fringe that assembles to communicate,
pick up, and protest without inhibition.
My canvas is twelve feet long—two feet wide, balanced on my crossed legs as
I sit and paint on top of a VW van. Eight feet of it—from left to right—
are fairly complete. (Tiny details will have to be finished in the studio.)
The remaining four feet are still completely empty.

May, 1970
Taos, New Mexico

Rick and the band are booked into a cantina at the edge of town. He's been writing a lot of songs lately and is more courageous about presenting them here. It must be a relief to have an enlightened audience— a change from the hardware convention he played at the Latin Quarter in New York City last month, which, he said, was like singing into a sea of pink feathers and can openers.

Dennis Hopper, who lives in Taos, came to the show last night. He invited Rick and me and the band out to his home—a large adobe built by Mabel Dodge Luhan in the twenties. His enthusiasm for this place is positively contagious. I want to see what he sees.

Mabel's house is spectacular—elegant—primitive. Now it's a commune of sorts. There are people every- where—cooking in the large kitchen—tending the livestock—gardening—contributing toward the editing of The Last Movie. *(The quarters beyond the garage and pigeon houses have been transformed into editing rooms.)*

As with most homes in New Mexico, the windows and doors are bordered on the exterior in turquoise blue to ward off evil spirits. On the upper two floors of the house, local Indians have painted the windows with designs on the inside, giving them the effect of stained glass. Homegrown grass was passed around like candy.

Later, after dinner, we decided to walk to town to buy a small sewing kit at Woolworth's, where a million different colors of thread waved at me from the notions counter.

I want to learn about this land which gives a sense of wellness and belonging—overwhelming relief— a connection to some deep level of consciousness.

This is the high desert where the Rio Grande snakes through a vast, purple valley. The river flows far below at the bottom of an enormous crevice, which splits the land at odd angles.

In the space of an hour, an early summer rain- storm thundered and flashed against the Sangres and left a double rainbow in its wake. Shadows raced across the desert floor as the sky returned to cobalt blue.

I've lived without the elements all my life and realize I've missed them. I'm going to stay a few days after the band moves on. The children are well cared for at home and there's much to learn here.

June, 1970
The musician came home this morning.

Silent partner in my bed
leave the great escape behind
the mindless faces of the road
are only sadness . . .
nevermind.

Worse by far's our forgotten dream
itself a strange illusion
or this poem misinterpreted
with quickly drawn conclusion.

It's Father's Day.
He was laughing in his sleep again.

THE TRAIN

1970

June, 1970 Father's Day

It's not possible to be all things for everybody. There's nothing left. This isn't like fifties television. There's a lot of pressure to keep the lid on. Two sets of parents encourage me to be my own person, but always within their limits. Their subtle message makes me feel trapped.

I must have been easily approved at seventeen—presentable—naive—unthreatening—moldable. But I'm older now and can think for myself. They suggest that if I'm to succeed within this marriage—it will be within the context of "the family."

His father looks at me warily and tells me to remember my responsibilities. (What responsibilities exactly? To my family? Or his family? Or to him?) His mother disapproves when my picture appears on a magazine cover using my first and last name—and not as "Mrs. Nelson."

Meanwhile, Rick could care less. He isn't part of this conspiracy. He's genuinely proud of anything I accomplish on my own.

Is reticence their secret of a compatible marriage?

June, 1970

I wanted to talk to my father. I thought he would understand. The desire to communicate with him overwhelmed the little voice that reminded me not to attempt sensitive disclosures "in person." And I forgot to have no expectations.

He stopped by the house in the late afternoon—his uneasiness instantly recognizable. I regretted that I'd asked him to meet with me. I was embarrassed for both of us.

His words of wisdom have always come in writing—when he's had time to think by himself without a needy daughter-in-crisis standing in front of him. I stammered around trying to explain why I was feeling anxious about my marriage—there was nothing wrong with it exactly, but why wasn't it everything I'd dreamed about? His response was blunt and to the point: "Get a divorce if you're so unhappy."

It was good advice, just not given with the most finesse. I wasn't ready to hear it anyway. I wanted him to understand me—comforting words—a hug. I wanted him to tell me he loved me.

But he was putting on his jacket and getting ready to leave. I followed him to the door.

". . . I'm not unhappy . . . Dad . . . claustrophobic, maybe . . . It's just that I find myself numb sometimes . . . somehow a threat . . . standing on nothing . . ."

"Bye, McGill," he said. And he was gone.

"In the deepest and most important things, we are unutterably alone."

Rainer Maria Rilke

A letter arrived from my father two days later. Just seeing his handwriting on the envelope brought a sense of well-being to me. His penmanship meant security—nothing could go wrong as long as my dad was around.

As always, he addressed me as "McGill," but as his emotions surfaced, he wrote in the third person—perhaps not wanting his feelings to make him appear vulnerable or weak.

His reassuring letter didn't disappoint. I read his words with great relief, knowing that he'd heard me—that his love was unconditional—and that he was trying hard to understand.

July, 1970
I came across this definition of "artist"
(or "artiste"): "a dreamer consenting to
dream of the actual world."

This dreamer is in constant battle with
her real life. She prefers escaping in
her head over the routine of everyday.
This sometimes is a dangerous thing.
I envy people who are content . . .
seemingly satisfied. Life seems much
less complicated for them.

Sari Heller wants me to have another
show in her gallery before Christmas.
I told her I wouldn't have time to paint
enough paintings by then. "Well," she
said, "just paint a variation of the same
thing over and over again—it doesn't
matter what—just paint quickly—
have an assembly line." I'd love to have
another show, but I need time to finish
enough paintings. It matters to me.

"To go into yourself and test the deeps in
which your life takes rise; at its source
you will find the answer to the question
whether you *must* create. Accept it,
just as it sounds, without inquiring into
it. Perhaps it will turn out that you are
called to be an artist. Then take that
destiny upon yourself and bear it, its
burden and its greatness, without ever
asking what recompense might come
from outside . . ."

Rainer Maria Rilke

June 25, 1970
I celebrate—an alien among friends—
at my birthday dinner in Venice. Am I
too old to be young?

Bow down to her on Sunday
Salute her when her birthday comes
Bow down to her on Sunday
Salute her when her birthday comes
For Halloween buy her a trumpet
For Christmas—give her a drum . . .

Bob Dylan

July, 1970 Laguna

A large group of family and friends lives within a quarter of a mile along Victoria Beach —my mother and father, Rick's aunt and uncle, our friends Joe and Camille, the Wicks, my sister Kelly, the Nelsons. We've spent many carefree, lost summer days here.

A year ago, our group had a potluck dinner so we could watch the moon landing together. My grandmother was worried our food would be ruined because we were more interested in watching man land on the moon than in our dinner being overcooked.

NANA
WAS WORRIED
THE MUSHROOMS
WOULD BURN

1970

*Honey crusted wheat bread
avocado, sprouts
the smell of Bain de Soleil
breeze off the ocean
late afternoon*

I cannot live with You—
It would be Life—
And Life is over there—
Behind the Shelf.

Emily Dickinson

LAGUNA THE FOURTH

1970

Would life be perfect if we always lived by the sea?

MY VERY BEST FRIEND

1970

"**S**eason after season, from 1952 right on through to 1966, they lived there in that solid, unpretentious house on that solid, unpretentious block . . . it was a comfortable, happy world."

David Handler on the Nelsons, *TV Guide*

"**R**icky Nelson, whose identity was being shaped by scripts written by his father, found the search for his identity far more difficult than an ordinary child would. What part of him was real? What part of him was the person in the script? Did he dare be the person he thought he was, or did that go too far outside the parameters of Ozzie's script?"

David Halberstam, *The Fifties*

"**M**en lead lives of quiet desperation."

Henry David Thoreau

September, 1970

Love has always meant a distant person to me—someone who isn't available or nurturing—someone who has difficulty communicating and expressing himself.

"SNOW BIRD"
KRISTIN NELSON 11-6-70

REASON TO BELIEVE—
"THE KIDS OF CAMP OAKLAND"
Kristin Nelson
7·3·70

THE KIDS OF CAMP OAKLAND

1970

October, 1970 Michigan

My sister asked me to paint Camp Oakland, a home for children in the Michigan woods. She wants to use the image on a Christmas card to raise money for the camp.

I realize that I've never seen the colors of fall—I thought primitive artists used wonderful imagination when they painted the trees deep shades of red, yellow, orange, violet, and chartreuse.

November, 1970

Feeling like a wife-in-the-way on his tour of the Armed Forces bases in England and Germany . . . this isn't exactly the way I'd dreamed of seeing Europe.

Asleep all day, up all night . . . dark, damp, depressing. We leave again in fifteen minutes . . . another long drive . . . another army base.

There's a coal strike . . . it's very cold. Electricity is turned off for six hours at a time and then the "lifts" in the hotel are inoperable. There's no one to share England with.

Just as everything closes for the evening, I awake and spend the hour before dark walking in the ancient cemetery across from the hotel. Reading by candlelight and no way to paint. Life is on hold.

The steel guitarist, particularly careful about his blow-dried comb-over, plugged his American hair dryer into a European socket and blew it up. He gets up early now and sits for hours in the window of his room, hoping to catch a breeze.

Hey let's go
All over the world
Rock and Roll girls
Rock and Roll girls

J. C. Fogerty

November, 1970

Last night
In a crowded West End pub
I watched two unknown faces
begin to know each other.
She spoke softly
Her hands touched his
and told him
of finer things.

From my position
I could only see his face
and he didn't really look like you
but there was something
the way his eyes listened
how he never quite managed
to shake the hair away from his forehead
but now that I think of it
It was the way his hands cared
as he held her
Then they left
and I was left
in a lonely room
in a crowded West End pub.

November, 1970

During the night, we travel into Wales—stopping periodically for the drummer to get sick by the side of the road. We're staying in a castle tonight and the band is very drunk. They won't care about the sheep on the rolling green hills or the church bells at dawn.

Four more days. I miss my kids. I miss my animals. I miss my studio. I miss my life.

HOME

December, 1970

I met Luci Johnson Nugent last summer when she came by the studio. She was nice, and very complimentary about the paintings. In particular, she liked Get Together *because she said it reminded her of her father's vision in the presidency— bringing together all the races.*

At some point, she must have discussed the painting with her family, because the president phoned this morning and asked me to ship it to the Johnson ranch in Austin, Texas, as a Christmas surprise for his daughter.

Helene Lindow—Luci's best friend—has commissioned a painting for her for this Christmas also. She's sent letters, information, and pictures of the Johnson ranch —photographs of the family and the hills of wildflowers that are Mrs. Johnson's passion.

April, 1971
My friend, John Longenecker,
asked me to be in a student film he was making
for his senior project at USC.

Tonight John's film,
The Resurrection of Broncho Billy,
with a production cost of nine hundred dollars,
won an Academy Award for
Best Live-Action Short of 1970.

It's about a cowboy's dreams
His old friend, Johnny Crawford, played Billy.
His old friend, Kris, played Billy's girl.

THE RESURRECTION
OF BRONCHO BILLY

1971

April, 1971

John Longenecker and I were in the reception area at Columbia Pictures by the Gower Street entrance. We were there waiting for a meeting to discuss Broncho Billy *when the Texas Kid walked in.*

My Town

I saw the Texas Kid today
He was old and bent
from many years
His shoes were worn
and one pant leg
hung down from the other

His pale hair was cut too short on one side
was he thinking of the old days?
I wonder—were they lovely and fine?
He'd forgotten to cut the remaining hair
or maybe
it was the drink that made him forget.

He's been in the business since '06
and Darryl F. Zanuck was his very best friend.

"You can't push around an old timer like me . . ."

The studio guard listened too fast
I was ashamed for him

"Well, Tex, if you care to leave your number . . ."

The Kid carried a scrapbook
a salute to the greatness that was Hollywood
memories of his famous friends
pictures of the Kid himself.

He slowly looked around
"I'll have a smoke and then I'll go . . ."

In his youth he would have left quickly
but age has numbed the rejection
and again he'll sit and wait
for the call that will never come.

THE TEXAS KID

1971

67

June

Dear Pa
 The day is beautiful - the beach is
warm and the air is clear and I'm
sitting in the sand and thinking about
you and me.
 Gunnar just ran up and opened his wet,
sandy fingers and handed me a tiny
shell. "It's for you" he said. Then he ran away.
 I thought about the cycle - a time for
everything - to learn, grow, move on, change,
to know, to love.
 Each of us is unique - our own person.
It's what I wish for my children and
what I hope you wish for me.
 I know I'm frustrating to you sometimes
because I'm not doing the things I should,
or rather, the things you think I should.
 I think about pleasing you in everything
I do. And more than anything, I want
you to be proud of me.
 I want to be courageous, kind -
to continue growing.
Change is good - it shouldn't be a thing
to fear.
It's healthy to question. How else do we
find answers?
 I want for you to understand me.
 I want for us to be friends.
 Happy Father's Day, Pa.
  Love always, Kris

June, 1971
Matthew couldn't find his drumsticks.
I asked where they were.
 "Gone with the wind," he said.

Dusty cold sunrise
sand fleas stirring on the beach
waves rolling ashore
retreating in anticlimax
early morning
 you on my mind

the sky gives promise
of a glorious day
anticipation.
we find common ground
in shells bordering the tide pools.

 you standing tall and straight
alone against the morning light
wind in your hair
blue eyes darker
than I remember.

sunshine

love

"**T**o be solitary, the way one was solitary
 as a child . . ."
 Rainer Maria Rilke

GUARDIANS OF THE ESTATE

1970

To Kelly—

In the sad mansion
with three dogs and a cat

my sister lives

wherever I may find her

You are golden
blue, pale, white
so very fragile

It's taken twenty-six years
for us to grow up
we are mothers now and
friends at last.

and you are beautiful
believing in white fences
the illusion of keeping the horses safe

have faith that
even though fences
no longer stand
the horses remain
on their own.

Kelly and me
and our future behind us,
Studio City, 1951

Tisha and me,
friends
through life.

August, 1971

We *were children again today. With*
flowers woven in our hair—costumed
in Renaissance finery from Tracy's big
costume trunk—my friend Tisha—her
daughter Heidi—and Tracy, Gunnar,
and Matt—went to the Pleasure Faire
in the Malibu Hills.

Music and laughter in the hot
afternoon—a barefoot day.

A gypsy promised that one day
I would marry a man who carried
a briefcase.

I know you know me well I say
'cause I'm the Palace Guard
Remember me? We made love today
At the king's bazaar

And you look at me with eyes that never see
I can feel something start to die inside of me

So before you show me everything
There's something you should know
I've worked with your friend, John the Geek
and his sidewalk travelin' show

I know your childhood tailored dreams
are very well disguised
So you don't have to fake it anymore
It's all been memorized

And you speak to me with feelings
as real as sealing wax
As the nearness dawns, the moth is gone,
Leaving trailless tracks.

Rick Nelson

SUNNY DAYS
I THOUGHT WOULD NEVER END

1971

CHAPTER THREE

1972–1980

TO BELIEVE
IN TOMORROW

1972

January, 1972

Part of me lives in the past, the rest lives for the future. Present time is spent pleasing everyone. Being an individual takes enormous amounts of effort.

I'm very protective of Rick. It's convenient trying to fix him, because then I don't have to fix me.

We had a "fifties" New Year's party and a chance to meet some new people. I'm reminded there's another world out there.

February, 1972

I look among my married friends hoping to find a glimmer of the discontentment I feel—and find none. They seem happy to insulate themselves by virtue of being married. What's the matter with me?

What's happened to the kindred spirit I shared with Rick? I suspect he's restless too, but after ten years of marriage, our censoring mechanisms have kicked in and we can't be completely honest about the unrest I suspect we share. Strange to think that the very communication that could bring us close again could damage the relationship beyond repair. It's a risk we don't take.

Still, there's something about his loneliness I understand. I think of us as soul spirits—old friends and partners. We continue to listen and grow—but— we've changed.

March, 1972

I remember the substance of our conversations—not the words. When I think of him, I see only the deepest blue.

Weary and hungry and fainting and sore
Fiends on the track of them
Fiends at the back of them
Fiends all around, but angels before
                Civil War lament

What's happened?

Did he change? Or did I? Or did we?

Maybe if I shut off the noise in my head, I'll stop looking outside to fill the empty place. We've decided to move to Laguna. Are we going home?

Our new home, an old and beautiful beach house, sits on top of a rocky cliff overlooking the Pacific. California poppies grow alongside exotic trees and cacti which are bent and twisted from the constant wind off the ocean. Tiny shells, sea glass, and leaves are imprinted into the footpaths winding to the sea, where a large fish has been crudely sculpted into the seawall.

> *Sitting in a vacant place*
> *a hummingbird with stylish grace*
> *faster then, than insects best*
> *he softened on a cotton nest*
> *his green, a shiny mallard hood*
> *with watchful eyes above he could*
> *behold us down below with caution*
> *in hopes we soon would be forgotten.*
> *the kids and I—to his dismay—*
> *were wonder-filled at his display*
> *cautiously, we whispered then*
> *and sought him just to be our friend*
> *we promised that this perfect tree*
> *would well respect his privacy*
> *a welcome guest to our new home*
> *two families by the sea alone.*

March, 1972

The story of the fish in the seawall was passed along by a neighbor. The house we live in was built by a sea captain. He was fishing off the rocks one day and his catch was light. As he reeled in his line, he hooked an enormous fish —a California catfish— the most beautiful fish he'd ever seen. Its yellow and orange scales glistened in the morning sun.

The fish was a scavenger —not a fish good for eating— the captain should have set it free, but he killed it instead. Overcome by this senseless act, he honored the fish by sculpting its likeness into the seawall. And he painted it gold like the sun.

The fish is flat blue now. I'd like to paint it back to its original color.

Once upon a time, there was a fisherman who lived with his wife in a hovel by the sea. One day he caught a large flounder. The flounder said, "Listen here, fisherman, let me live. I'm not a real flounder but an enchanted prince . . ."

The fisherman put the flounder back.

"Husband," asked the wife, "didn't you catch anything today?"

"Only a flounder who said he was an enchanted prince, so I let him go," said the fisherman.

"Didn't you wish for anything?" said the wife.

"No," said the fisherman. "What should I have wished for?"

"Ah!" said the wife. "Don't you think that it's awful that we've got to live in this hovel? You should have wished for a cottage. Now go do it!"

"Flounder, flounder in the sea
Prithee, harken unto me
My wife, Isobel, must have her own will
and so I beg a boon of thee."

"Well, what do you want?" asked the flounder.

"My wife doesn't want to live in a hovel, she wants a cottage," said the fisherman.

"Just go home," said the flounder. "She's already got it."

The Brothers Grimm

April, 1972

Rick was up all night again—pacing until dawn. He retunes his guitar— smokes cigarettes down to their filters and places them on end. He'll sleep through Easter Sunday and make a first appearance in the terry robe at dusk, when the cycle will start over.

The children have been up since dawn and hunted for eggs without him. They're accustomed to their father's sleeping through the days. I'll never get used to it.

*Sometimes it's hard
to be everything for everybody
they tear at me in bits and pieces
I'm weary at times
sad from many things
Am I supposed to lead an incidental
   life?
I wonder if this is all.
How can I find the strength to leave?
I'm alone in this—
I let it happen.*

Neither of us had much of a chance to be anything outside of our parents' best intentions.

May, 1972

He never learned how to change a diaper, doesn't understand how to write a check, and is amused by it all. I realize I've been carefully groomed and approved to take over for his father, who was caretaker before me.

But I want my own life.

When he was a kid, inarticulateness was part of his charm. He's thirty-two now and being irresistible doesn't get him as far.

I don't want to be this angry.

Fallen away from my best right self . . . got lost somehow . . . the song of the starved soul . . .

"[D]on't you think we need to conserve our energies—emotions and feelings— for what we are going to make the big things in our lives instead of letting so much run away on the little things every day[?]"

Georgia O'Keeffe

I have a mansion
but forget the price
I've never been there
They tell me it's nice

I live in hotels
tear out the walls
I have accountants
who pay for it all

They say I'm crazy
but I have a good time
I'm just looking for clues
at the scene of the crime
Life's been good to me, so far . . .

My Maserati
does one eighty-five
I lost my license
now I don't drive . . .

I have a limo
ride in the back
I lock the doors
in case I'm attacked

I make hit records
My fans, they can't wait
they write me letters
tell me I'm great

So I got me an office
gold records on the wall
Just leave a message
maybe I'll call

Lucky I'm sane
after all I've been through
Everybody says I'm cool
He's cool

I can't complain
but sometimes I still do
life's been good to me
So far . . .

I go to parties
sometimes until four
It's hard to leave
when you can't find the door

Life's been good to me—
so far . . .

Joe Walsh

82

June, 1972

Driving down Laguna Canyon Road, the boys were in the backseat.

Matthew was singing impressively loudly—something about a "gopher in a tree and then the farmer cried and then it went away . . ."

When he stopped singing, he said, "You like it, Mom?"

"Very good, Matt," I said.

"I made it up!" he said.

A few minutes later, Gunnar, not to be outdone, started singing "The Farmer in the Dell."

He sang it straight through—start to finish—beginning with "the farmer takes a wife" to "the cheese stands alone . . . hi ho the dairyo . . ." etc.

"You like it, Mom?" he asked.

"Yes, Gunn . . . that was very good."

"I made it up," he said.

July, 1972

Fifty guests helped to celebrate the Fourth of July at the beach house. Three big grills were set up on the sand to barbecue kabobs and corn on the cob. The fireworks began after dark. Tracy was terrified of the noise, while the boys couldn't wait for the next big bang.

Then the wife said, "Listen, husband, the cottage is too cramped. I want a larger house. Go back to the flounder and ask him to give us a castle."

The husband's heart grew heavy and he didn't want to go; nevertheless, he went. When he got to the sea, the water was purple, gray, and dense, although it was still calm . . .

The Brothers Grimm

boB BY Matthew
7-10-19 73

August, 1972

How do I explain to my children that this is not the real world—that life isn't all instant gratification, celebrity, and smothering attention? They're so young to understand. We're surrounded by well-meaning friends and relatives whose very existence seems to depend on protecting the lie of the perfect family. They encourage a sense of entitlement in my children. I want the kids to know that a good heart and peace within is far more important than fame or material possessions.

November, 1972

I don't think I was the only one to confuse fiction with fact. When I grew up I wanted to be just like Harriet. On the Nelson show, there wasn't any problem that couldn't be solved within thirty minutes. Unlike any family I knew, the Nelsons listened to their children. If the boys resented their parents' authority, they did so politely and with humor. They worked everything out in a peaceful way and were demonstrative with one another.

Now, after ten years, I realize they're as human as the rest of us. His brother, the outgoing one and easily his mother's favorite, stretches the truth with ease. Rick and his father have major arguments about most everything. His mother doesn't bake apple pies and she has a vodka with vermouth before dinner.

Harriet says that my mother-image of her is a myth. She says to knock it off with all my expectations and reminds me that I'll never be like her because she isn't like her.

Cinderella and the prince
lived, they say, happily ever after,
like two dolls in a museum case
never bothered by diapers or dust,
never arguing over the timing of an egg,
never telling the same story twice,
never getting a middle-aged spread,
their darling smiles pasted on for eternity.
Regular Bobbsey Twins.
That story.

Anne Sexton

February, 1973

Rick agreed to headline a Rock and Roll Revival at Madison Square Garden on the condition that the promoters take out the word Revival and replace it with Show. Revival, *he says, makes him feel like he's died.*

He hasn't made a career out of singing oldies. He's worked hard at his music, written new songs, and formed the Stone Canyon Band. He feels he can reach a different audience by playing this venue.

And so it was called a "Rock and Roll Show." But the people who'd come to see their fifties icons lived in a time warp and didn't want their heroes to grow up. It was positively frightening.

Bobby Rydell, who'd lost his pompadour in a big way, opened the show and Chuck Berry followed with a self-impersonation. The performers hadn't changed musically —they just looked older. After intermission, Rick came on stage with the Stone Canyon Band.

The crowd took one look at all that long hair, heard the sound of "Honky Tonk Woman," and began to stomp and boo and whistle. It sounded like a tidal wave.

Rick stopped playing. The color drained from his face before he managed to walk offstage, the band close behind.

It was deathly quiet in the dressing area. I asked why we didn't leave. He was using a towel to wipe the sweat off his face and I asked again if we could go. He explained that he'd been told George Harrison and Bob Dylan were in the audience and he wanted to wait for them, in case they came back to say hello. But they never did.

At home the next day, he went into his den and wrote "Garden Party," his first million seller in a long time.

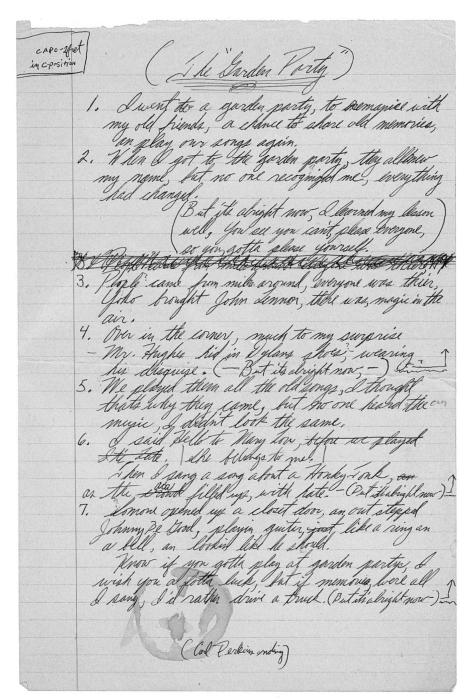

Lyrics by
Rick Nelson

"**F**lounder, flounder in the sea
Prithee, harken unto me
My wife, Isobel, must have her own will
And so I beg a boon of thee."

"Well, what does she want?" said the flounder.

"Oh," said the fisherman, "she wants to live in a stone castle."

"Just go home, she's already waiting at the gate," the flounder said.

When he went home, his wife was standing on the great stone steps.

"Come inside," she said, taking his hand.

"Well," said the wife, "isn't this beautiful?"

"Yes," said the husband. "Hopefully it will stay this way. Now let's live in the beautiful castle and be content."

"We'll have to think about that," said the wife, "and sleep on it."

The Brothers Grimm

April, 1973

When he's not on the road, he paces until dawn, says the waves disturb his sleep. He eats bowls of ice cream, smokes cigarettes, and investigates phantom noises in the dark.

Fog hovers over the coastline. A lethargy has set in. There's no energy or inspiration—no paintings. Moving to Laguna was a huge mistake. This house won't save us.

May, 1973

Every day I pray for the concentration to paint. Then I drive to Los Angeles and look at houses for sale.

We put the beach house on the market and will be moving back to LA soon.

"**E**ven the most repressed woman has a secret life, with secret thoughts and secret feelings which are lush and wild, that is, natural. Even the most captured woman guards the place of the wildish self, for she knows intuitively that someday there will be a loophole, an aperture, a chance, and she will hightail it to escape."

Clarissa Pinkola Estés

June, 1973   New Mexico

There's a small adobe on the northbound side of Highway 25, halfway between Albuquerque and Santa Fe. In the dirt yard, a blinking neon sign reads PALMS READ.

A barefoot woman in braids and a yellow dress turns my hand over.

"You have many enemies," says the woman. "You must pay me more money and I will pray for you . . . I will light a candle."

*Promise me a rainbow
crystal mountains
daydreams
a loyalty nothing can shake
absolute trust
a love that is whole
and true*

yes

We've moved to a farmhouse in the foothills of Studio City. I'm back where I was born. The children are happy here —it's a relief for everyone. With renewed energy, I've scheduled another art show, but this time at the Anahalt Gallery on La Cienega. It'll run through the month of December.

IN OUR OWN WAY,
TO BE FREE

"IN OUR OWN WAY, TO BE FREE"
KEITH NELSON
2-5-75

"ONCE IT SNOWED ON SUNSWEPT DRIVE"
KRISTIN NELSON
6-20-73

June, 1973

A *cautious, first attempt at a memory painting.*

"**. . . Q**uiet and hidden beginnings of something personal . . ."
Rainer Maria Rilke

June, 1973

P*ieces of the puzzle fill in slowly and take shape—one memory—one painting at a time. I've been afraid to go back, although I don't know why. Whatever my apprehension—it hasn't diminished through the years. But I'm ready to allow for enlightenment—I remember great times when I was little.*

Memory: It is 1948. My sister is a baby and it's snowing in Los Angeles! The wood-paneled walls in the living room are glowing from the light of the fire. My father loads his camera, and my mother and grandmother dress me warmly. I have a red coat, mittens, and rain boots. The neighborhood is covered in white and the snow is soft and cold. I bring charcoal from the barbecue for the snowman's eyes. I'm three years old.

Roger and me,
1948

July, 1973

Horses running free
carrot cake and strawberries
warm red wine
wind in the grass

guests gathered to listen
as Ken and Tere married
the best man knew Buddy Holly
his wife wore a low-cut dress

and over there
in red overalls
and a white sweater
she spoke with a French accent
on a hot summer day

some were smiling
bridging the creek
some fell in

bright promises
were made
under the maypole
horses running free

FIELD AND DREAM

1973

"FIELD AND DREAM"
KUSTIN NELSON
7-12-73

91

ROCK AND ROLL LULLABY

1973

When I was a little girl
I'd put my dolls to bed
I'd dress them all differently
and kiss them on the head

Their sheets were made of tissue
fine and clean and white
with folded cloth to cushion
their dreams throughout the night

I'd make sure they'd say their prayers
to the Father, God the Son
you know, back then, at times I'd feel
my work was never done

but the days grew into months and years
and still I tell myself
that once my family's tucked in bed
I'll have some carefree days ahead
When I can spend some lovely time
painting my pictures
or finishing this rhyme

July, 1973

In some form, the dream comes almost every night—my childhood home of many secrets:

In the version of the dream I had last night, my sister and I are identically dressed. We share the same bedroom, twin canopy beds, the same haircut, the same dreaded bangs. We are polite Catholic girls, although the nuns that make me contrary have made her complaisant. No matter our differences, my sister and I share a mutual disadvantage in our mother's eyes—we know we'll never be the quarterback she'd hoped for. Still, we seek her attention as if our lives depended on it and we compete and argue our way through childhood and adolescence, where no confidence is safe.

I wake up from the dream . . . or have I been dreaming?

August, 1973
The illusive boundaries between fact
and fiction can be confusing for a kid
born on the outskirts of Hollywood.
Nothing was as it seemed.

Yes
She said laughing
with violet dreams turned away at dusk
through terry cloth slippers
and tuna fish casseroles
her remarkable talent once applauded
appreciated
she gave away secrets
to her lover only

Now
with the years comes refinement
and grace
practiced, invisible
quite astonishing, really

but before morning
alone in the dark
rage escapes the room
the solitary window
the sky the color of muted light
oh, the injustice that age brings
this fine-boned beauty

She listens to the familiar voice
soothes herself
encouragements from the depths
Her trademark eyes
so attractive in an offsetting way
have dissolved to wrinkled distractions

How tiresome it all becomes

After all
the mask's a professional one
and dishonesty becomes her so
by noon

WORKING IT OUT

1973

September, 1973

My little brother and I are good friends.
Being "the son of" is difficult for any
child and it has been hard on my brother.
But as I see it, the pressure to excel is
self-imposed. Mark is a perfectionist to
the point of rigidity at times.

    He excelled in football at UCLA. He
broke school records and his collarbone
and shoulder. Now, he says, he's thinking about being an actor.

Nobody knows how much he hurts
I've never heard him complain
He'll tell you that's the way it is
No problem, just the game.

But when his final race is run
after his final days are done
I look into his clear blue eyes
and sometimes there is no surprise

I can see his pain
just a little bit
Not enough to stop or quit
But is the game the thing? I wonder
or just his way, my little brother

96

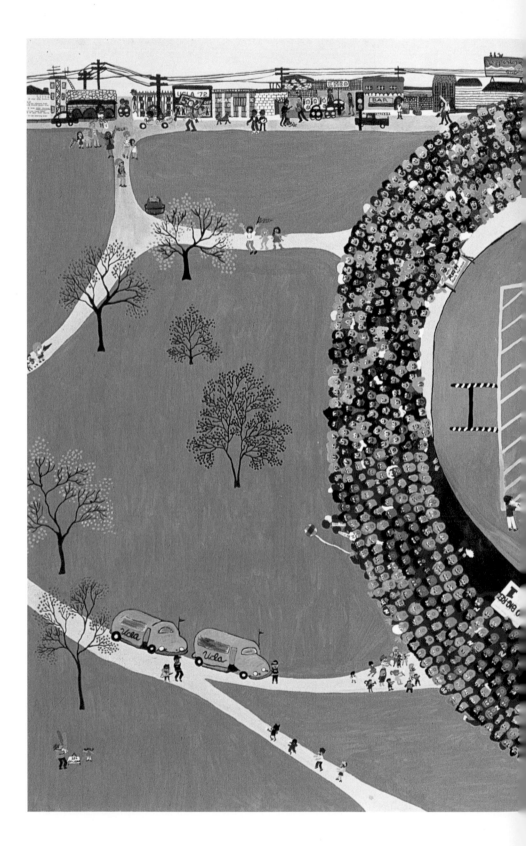

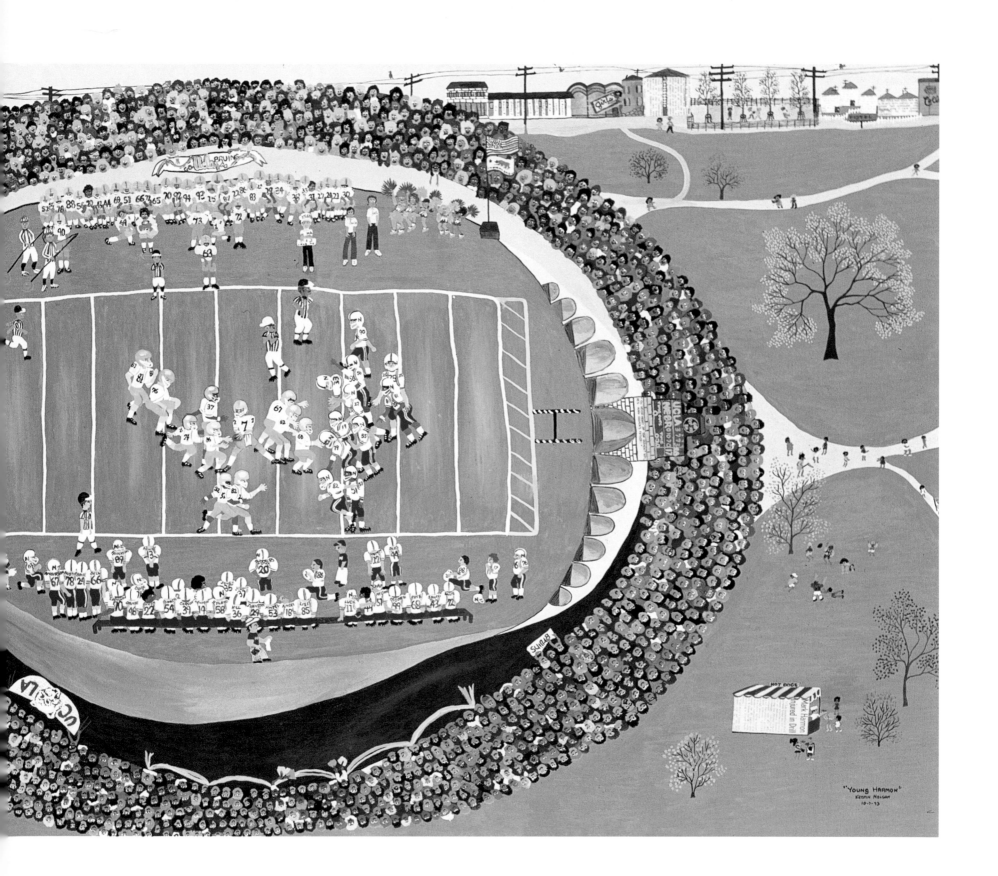

YOUNG HARMON

1973

Luci Johnson Nugent

2313 RED RIVER STREET
AUSTIN, TEXAS 78705

September 24, 1973

Dear Kris,

Helene sent me a delightful article that appeared in the "New York Times" about your families "farm", and I thoroughly enjoyed gaining an insight into the loves of your life. Speaking of loves of your life brings me to your request for Walter Barnes to take color slides of the two paintings of yours that I own. I am very pleased to comply with your request and have made an appointment to meet with Mr. Barnes on September 26th for the photograph session.

You certainly have my permission to utilize the transparencies in your catalogue as your paintings have surely been a great source of joy for us, and we would love to share that pleasure with others.

Your second request is one that sparks a nostalgic mood for me, for your "Get Together" or "Ring Around the World" as you well know, is a painting that I believe beautifully portrays what Lyndon Johnson was all about. I know he felt that it was surely all about what he tried to do - as we already have a colored slide of it, one he had taken to make a print for his personal Head Start School

in Stonewall. Thus, I am elated and honored that you have requested permission to have it appear on the UNICEF calendar, for you couldn't have been more right in assuming that its "reprinting for such a good cause" would please me - as it surely does!

Your understanding that I might not feel comfortable in honoring your request and your insight that all this was optional made me far more eager - "I would have been anyway." Your sensitivity and your humility makes it a joy to do business with you.

I hope that your show is a grand success, and now I'm going to turn the tables and make a few requests of my own. I would like very much to see or purchase, whichever is possible, a copy of the catalogue of your work when it is completed, and also a copy of the UNICEF calendar.

By the way, where is your showing going to take place - as I wish it might be feasible for me to see personally what you've been up to lately?

Again, as always, please know that both of your paintings have brought an immense amount of happiness to all the "Nugent's Nest", and to those we love.

Devotedly,

Luci

November, 1973

Four weeks until the opening of my show. In my mind, I envision myself a storyteller—a story painter—a documentarian who uses color in place of words—when actually what I am— is someone's tired wife—the queen of distraction.

Nothing touches me quite like a note written in my grandmother's careful Austrian hand.

Dear Kris a Rick

Thankyou, Thankyou I never seen such beutiful Flowers. You spent much to much money on me Kris, I hope your Mother will paint them beefor the are gone if she has time.

Much love to you and Rick.
Nana

RED FLOWERS (Wild Flowers, Future Dream)

1971

FRIEDA AND LAWRENCE IN TAOS
REMEMBER AND BE GLAD.
KRISTIN NELSON 11-6-73

Promise me
you'll walk above the noise
and find your inner light
let it grow
like a sunflower
and at 92
a young woman
will look through your eyes
and cry a little
for something so pure and whole
in a world with so much wrong
                              Douglas Wick

Back, behind us,
the dignified, tall firs begin.
Bluish, associating with their shadows,
a million Christmas trees stand
waiting for Christmas.
                              Elizabeth Bishop

REMEMBER AND BE GLAD:
FRIEDA AND LAWRENCE
IN TAOS

1973

December, 1973

Preview reception tomorrow night. The paintings are hung in the gallery. We're expecting again in August and we have decided the baby's name will be Sam.

December, 1973
Second One-Woman Show

I walked in late—scared and full of self-doubt, certain this time that I'd failed and that these paintings would confirm the first show was a fluke. No amount of reassurance helps. It feels like my soul is on view.

I painted the Nelsons' Hollywood home as it was in 1943, and Rick's solitary childhood made a sad and unintentional appearance.

WHITE GATES

1973

Does man love Art? Man visits Art, but squirms.
Art hurts. Art urges voyages—
and it is easier to stay at home,
the nice beer ready.

Gwendolyn Brooks

1822, CAMINO PALMERO
HOLLYWOOD, 1943

1973

February, 1974

We're living in Studio City, but the merry-go-round and ponies are gone from Ventura Boulevard and so is the dress shop with the bridal gowns and the fabric store with the glittered material that reminded me of Cinderella.

Fire trails, inhabited by deer, coyotes, birds, raccoons, and an occasional mountain lion, wind through the mountains in back of our house. We have a small barn, where I've brought my childhood horse, Socks, to live out his days. He shares the corral with Rick's quarter horse, Moon, and Tracy's pony, Rootbeer. The children have goats and rabbits and I planted a vegetable garden. I can make it work.

The next morning the wife woke up first. "Husband," she said. "Wake up and look at the countryside. Go to the flounder and tell him you want to be King of the Country."

"I don't want to be King of the Country," said the husband.

"Then go to him and tell him that I want to be king," said the wife.

The man did not want to ask the flounder, but still he did. The sea was gray and black and twisting and turning.

"Flounder, flounder in the sea
Prithee, harken unto me
My wife, Isobel, must have her own will
And so I beg a boon of thee."

The Brothers Grimm

We all have reasons
for moving.
I move
to keep things whole.
Mark Strand

September, 1974

Our fourth child was born on August 29. His name is Sam Hilliard and he is as beautiful as his dad. Rick had emergency gall bladder surgery two days after the baby was born, so we're a couple of invalids for a while.

Something
fragile,
something
rare.

December, 1974

Christmas carols send me into a catatonic stupor—I can't face the holidays. There aren't enough hours in the day. Rick's on the road until Christmas, and with four children I can't find help—an incredibly busy time.

Christmas Eve, 1974

I forgot the kids' letters to Santa and phoned the toy store in a panic. The staff there assured me they had the children's requests and said to pick the toys up later tonight—that they'd even be gift wrapped.

The toys were indeed wrapped—all of them—but not one was labeled. I finished rewrapping and labeling at dawn.

Dear Kris,

I love you and need you very much. I'm so sorry for causing you so much unhappiness. I really didn't mean to.

I just want you to know what a very special person you are. Again I'm sorry if I've caused you to have any selfdoubts because you really shouldn't have any.

I guess its always been hard for me to show you or tell you how much I care, but I really do. I love you very much

Me

The recent period of my life has been the start of a new cycle for me. It is the start of gaining of a very positive feelings

...know that I have to feel good about myself before I'm able to share those feelings with anyone else.

Feelings of nothingness can be an overwhelming thing to overcome. Sometimes I feel I am a spectator watching myself from the outside

From
Rick's journal

February, 1975

Terrible news. After months of pain, Rick's father had exploratory surgery and has been diagnosed with cancer of the liver. He's been given less than six months to live.

May, 1975

We're told it won't be much longer now. His body, so fit last summer, is now impossibly thin. A tube down his throat is causing him great discomfort. He's the strength of the family—how can he be dying? As always, people see Rick and ask, "How're your mom and dad?" And usually he'll answer "fine," except lately when he adds, "Well, my father's not feeling so good." And the people will continue smiling as if they hadn't heard—don't want to hear.

His father is home now as he wished to be, with his family by his side. He drew Rick close tonight and whispered a favorite Vince Lombardi quote in his ear: "Weakness makes cowards of us all."
 With each day, his blue eyes fade and death is near.

June, 1975

My father gave Ozzie's eulogy. It's so sad. Harriet seems to be holding up—Rick is even quieter than usual—smoking too much—suffering from insomnia. This is a reckoning of enormous proportions.

August, 1975

Ordinarily, music would save him. Rick is a musician before anything else—a fact generally overlooked because of early fame as a teenage idol. He doesn't talk about it, but it's a source of great frustration. The unacceptance of his peers eats away at his soul.

November, 1975

Rain makes everything easier. Mist outside the window —a stillness through the canyon—a bird cries in the woods. I'm alone next to him as he sleeps. He's numb these days and life seems so painful for him. He doesn't mention his father.

January, 1976

Our marriage is a combination of laughter and despair. He's become so defensive. I'm left out of decisions now. He hired a new "manager" out of nowhere. I question the guy's qualifications. Where does he come from? What's his experience? Rick, a master of revealing as little information as possible lately, tells me he's Colonel Parker's adopted son—as if that means anything. I think the guy's a complete creep. After so many years, Rick and I are strangers. There are no paintings.

April, 1976

I didn't get out of bed today.

May, 1976

Strangling in convention—dying of indifference. Blaming him for what's wrong with me.

June, 1976

Under the covers again. Rick's Uncle Don is over here a lot lately—standing around downstairs with his perfect manhattan. I can't stand it—I can't stand it—I can't stand it!

July, 1976

I found a job. I'm apprenticing for a literary agent. It's so nice to be self-sufficient—to slip silently away.

The rock 'n' roll wife
is always alone
She makes solemn promises
If he calls
she won't answer
and he'll care
she's not home
but
the long night's begun
and
it's dark
in her room

"Well, what does she want?" asked the flounder.

"Oh," said the man, "she wants to be king."

"Go back home," said the flounder. "She's already king."

"Oh, wife," said the fisherman, "now you are king. Let's not wish for anything more."

"Yes," she said. "Now I am king. But now I must become emperor as well."

The husband went again to ask the flounder for his wife to be emperor. But as he walked along, he became scared and thought to himself, This won't turn out well at all. When he got to the sea, it was black and dense.

The Brothers Grimm

109

August, 1976
A *time of believing again—*
of hope and promise—a time
of intense feelings. He sends
a telegram from the road.

NO TIME TO WRITE. I WILL GET BACK LATE SATURDAY NITE. REMEMBER A WIRE CAN BE WONDERFUL—I LOVE YOU. NO SGD

Will *you save me September?*

There's a kid on the steps
with a mouth like yours
he looked twice
the way you first looked at me
but his eyes were dull
unseeing
and when I looked again
you weren't there

I'm always amazed
that I forget
the deepest blue
softest skin
tenderest touch
moments
that made me cry

> **T**hen I said softly to myself—
> "That must have been the Sun!"
> Emily Dickinson

> **T**hen wear the gold hat, if that will move her;
>   If you can bounce high, bounce for her too,
> Till she cry "Lover, gold-hatted, high bouncing lover,
>   I must have you!"
>
>   F. Scott Fitzgerald
>   (Thomas Parke D. Invilliers)

May, 1977

We have flown to Paris to meet up with Tracy, who's at the end of a school excursion through England, Wales, Italy, and France. Rick and I are friendly, but the silences speak loudly again. A few drawings in my sketchbook.

June, 1977

Before traveling back to California, Rick stopped in Washington, D.C., for a show in Baltimore. We had taken the Concorde from Paris and arrived in Washington on schedule. But he was hours late for his performance and the opening act had to improvise while everyone waited for him to show up. The promoters were understandably upset. Rick was apathetic. He didn't offer excuses or apologies.

I talked to him again about r-e-s-p-o-n-s-i-b-i-l-i-t-y and the importance of boundaries to the creative framework, and it dawned on me that I've been talking to myself all these years. I thought about time wasted and the ways I'd rather be spending it right now.

I had so much I wanted to do—so many plans—how did I become a warden instead? A broken record of a wife who sounds a lot like his father?

The angel is barely
speaking   to me
Once in a horn of light
he stood   or someone like him
salutations in gold-leaf
ribboning from his lips
Today again   the hair streams
to his shoulders
the eyes reflect   something
like a lost country   or so I think
but the ribbon has reeled itself
up
   he isn't giving
or taking any shit
We glance miserably
across the room   at each other

It's true   there are moments
closer and closer together
when words stick   in my throat
              'the art of love'
              'the art of words'
I get your message Gabriel
just   will you stay looking
straight at me
awhile longer

Adrienne Rich

September, 1977

I won't go on the road again. I don't find trashing rental cars or hitting each other with shaving cream pies as amusing as he does. I don't want to be around any of them. The rock 'n' roll lifestyle gets old fast and so do I.

January, 1978 Santa Fe

A friend and I have been talking about a story idea—a crossroads of sorts— that takes place in New Mexico at the turn of the century. We've been doing research in the archives in Santa Fe and are going to attempt to write a screenplay together.

Dreams of a creative life have been lost in so many years of minutiae. I forget how it feels to be passionate and inspired about a project.

"And when what is near you is far, then your distance is already among the stars and very large; rejoice in your growth, in which you naturally can take no one with you, and be kind to those who remain behind . . ."

Rainer Maria Rilke

Over the writing table
it is sunset
a sky with pink clouds
growing dark

ivy in the coffee can

like stars
other lights come on
from secret places
one by one
they open into the night

June, 1978 Los Angeles
Last Little League game of the season. Score tied. Bottom of the seventh. Two out. Matthew Nelson up to bat. He hits a triple. Gunnar Nelson up to bat. He gets a base hit and in slides Matt with the winning run. Matt trots toward the dugout—"Nice one!" I say. "I'm dependable," he responds.

August, 1978
I'm the constant—the disciplinarian— the rock—the mom—exhausted. Struggling with my writing partner, the screenplay, and self-esteem. I don't know if we'll ever get this story written.

October, 1978
Rick's manager is extremely bad news.

November, 1978
Not thinking clearly and full of distractions . . . maybe if we moved again?
Rick's found a 7,000-square-foot house that was built by Errol Flynn in the Hollywood Hills. The house for sale is the main house of a sixteen-acre parcel called Mulholland Farm. These days, Rick fancies himself as Errol Flynn.

"**G**o back home," said the flounder. "She's already emperor."

The husband saw that the entire castle was now made of polished marble and alabaster. Soldiers marched in front, blowing trumpets and beating drums.

"Oh, wife," he said, "it's good that you are now emperor."

"Husband," she said, "why are you standing there? Go tell the flounder that I want to be like God."

"I can't do that," said the man.

"Go!" commanded his wife. "I'm the emperor and you're just my husband. You do as I say!" And the man went, filled with dread and fear.

The horizon was completely red, as if a thunderstorm was coming. The man stepped forward filled with dread:

"Flounder, flounder in the sea
Prithee, harken unto me
My wife, Isobel, must have her own will
And so I beg a boon of thee . . ."

"What does she want?" said the flounder.
"She wants to be like God," said the man.
"Go back home. She's sitting in the hovel again."
And there she sits . . .

The Brothers Grimm

Nana and me,
1946

February, 1979

__M__y grandmother is back in the hospital —she looks so sweet lying all in pink— wide-eyed, staring at the ceiling. Today, she doesn't worry about cooking a next meal or a great-grandchild with a runny nose. She says that her room is nice. Is she thinking about a new recipe? Lawrence Welk? That she knows she's dying?

It's so quiet here.

Her thoughts come randomly: "You know, Krist, I'm sorry I have this opera- tion to go through . . ."

She's the wisest woman I've ever known. I take her hand and can't imagine life without her. After a while, when I think she's sleeping, I quietly get up to go. She opens her eyes and looks at me.

"Krist," she says,

Johanna Preyer (daughter from Anna Eichinger)
Franz Wenzlgasse 2
2231 Strasshof
Austria   29.9.8o

Dear Elyse,

     Thank you for informing us about Aunt Mina's passing,
please let us condole with you sincerely, I am sure you
will miss your good Mother very much. We are very sad too
though we had to expect her passing after what she had
written in her last letter to Mother and I do hope you
were able to soothe the pains she wrote from.

I am sure she was very happy to live in your family and
she always wrote what a good daughter you were. She was
a great lady indeed, in her was such a lot of kindness.
She did so much for us, especially in the difficult years
after the war, though she hardly did know us as she was a
child when she left Austria and her experiences here were
not the best ones I expect. What a lot of dresses she sent
us, the first watch I had she sent me, hidden into a parcel
of rice, and still today a lot of things around us reminds
us of her. We always shall bear her in minds.

It would be very nice if you could come over to Austria
one day, you are very welcome.
Mother is 73 years now and her health is not very good,
she is suffering from the heart, blood-pressure and
circulation, the eyes (cataract) etc. Some five years ago
we wanted to give her the money for going to see Aunt Mina,
but she didn't want, she is very afraid of flying. The
brothers of Aunt Mina are 75 and 76 now.
Of course we shall inform all the relatives about Aunt
Mina's passing; we shall send some flowers, please put
them on her grave.

Please excuse my bad English, I learnt it at school but
I never had much chance to practice it an so I forgot it.

I do hope we shall meet one day.

                              Much love

                                 from

                              Hanne   and Mother

"You must paint and paint—it's your life."

Love Nana

March, 1979

We've moved to the Flynn house. The infamous two-way mirror remains over the master bed. The room has also been wired for camera and sound. There are spy holes in the ceilings and walls and secret escape routes. Strange-smelling cologne wafts through the upstairs bath. The faucets turn by themselves, the windows open on their own. Is Errol making his presence known here? Why did I think this place would fix anything?

"The place seemed tangled and matted with emotion."
Virginia Woolf

August, 1979

This is the house where death began. I don't paint. I don't have any desire to paint. I've moved upstairs with the children and at night I drink too much. I'm terrified to sleep. If Rick is home, he lives in his walk-in closet in the white terry robe. The manager brings his every request to the bathroom window. People come and go in the middle of the night. Do they think I don't see—can't hear? What does it matter? I do nothing about it.

We are in serious trouble. My family won't support me. In their eyes, Rick's a really nice guy—a celebrity. There's nothing wrong with "Nice Handsome Rick," as my mother calls him. She tells me I'm the one with the problem. She doesn't understand why I'd want to leave this marriage.

September, 1980

Someone took off the training wheels—let go of the safety net. Watching him self-destruct is the most painful thing in the world.

November 18, 1980

Dear Rick,

I haven't talked to you all week. I try to understand your need to be away so much because I know you never got a chance to be a kid when you were growing up. But it doesn't make the responsibility of our family any easier on me. It's just, I can't do it all anymore.

I didn't get much of a chance to have an adolescence, either. Our marriage was good for a long time because we loved each other and because we were able to communicate. I handled everything and was glad to do so. I was able to paint and I had a sense of accomplishment, too. I felt you appreciated me and that made everything worthwhile.

But I'm fooling myself now.

I've asked you to get help with me so many times. You agree for the moment and then sleep through the doctor's appointments. Are you happy with the way things are?

I need you to be a husband and a father. I can't do it all anymore—I'm so tired. Please talk to me.

love,

Kris

December, 1980

I guess I've had an answer.
He doesn't respond.
He doesn't do anything at all.
So many hurts.
I'm dying of indifference and
think less and less of him—
and of myself.
If he's not on the road, he spends time in the big closet
or at his desk in the den
putting together a small model airplane
barefoot, smoking, in the white terry robe.
I have to think of the children and of myself first for once.
He asked me to stay through Christmas.
Then it's time to go.
Silence and rage isn't healthy for anyone.
Nobody to the rescue this time.

Recurring Dream:

The Sunswept house has become *our honeymoon house,* but now

it's cantilevered off the top of the mountain.

"You must not be from here,"

I say to my grandmother, who takes me from room to room.

"I'm from Vienna," she says, smiling.

Our dogs have become old dogs.

They're fed from dishes placed on shelves. Rick is here.

The master bedroom is decorated from the sixties.

We make plans to take out the walls and paint the interior white. But the east side of the house is the Flynn house

and *damp earth* piles up to the windows.

There's a gaping hole in the floor and

ominous light

from a single bulb.

117

CHAPTER FOUR

1981–1987

THE DAY
AFTER CHRISTMAS

1980

January, 1981
My daughter said, "You know, Mom—
one day he's going to wake up and find
us all gone. It's already too late for me."
It's too late for all of us.

Eighteen years together
we'll go on separately for the better
that was the plan
wasn't that the plan?

I wish only the best for you
I've loved you all my life
but the blindfold's off
this time for good
I've made myself look at me
time to find lost integrity

I'll take this chance
leaving home
been alone for too long

How easily the plan forms

quietly,

catlike

I'm gone

January, 1981

It's hard to know what makes a marriage fall apart—
the disillusionment and bitterness—the breakdown in
communication. What were once life celebrations have
given way to deep despair.

> **S**o you live from day to day
> And you dream about tomorrow
> And the hours go by like minutes
> And the shadows come to stay
> So you take a little something
> To make them go away.
> > Don Henley / Glenn Frey

February, 1981

I've always been a casual drinker—it was no big deal—
it was fun—a way to relax and think myself more witty
and clever than I was. Now, quietly, I don't drink for
fun anymore. Alcohol numbs—renders me unconscious
enough to sleep for a little while—until the next day
begins all over again—with a crashing headache—more
deeply depressed than the day before.

March, 1981

A friend found a job for me with a steady paycheck.
I'm assisting a casting director for $200 a week. I moved
out with the boys into a tiny two-bedroom valley rental.
Tracy wants to stay in the big house with Rick.

> **Y**our mind now, moldering like wedding-cake,
> heavy with useless experience, rich
> with suspicion, rumor, fantasy,
> crumbling to pieces under the knife-edge
> of mere fact. In the prime of your life.
> Nervy, glowering, your daughter
> wipes the teaspoons, grows another way.
> > Adrienne Rich

May, 1981

The responsibility of supporting myself and the children is
overwhelming—I don't make enough to afford child care
and don't have the skills for a better-paying job. There
are black spaces and large amounts of time that I can't
account for. Tubes of paint dry up in the basket by the
back door.

June, 1981

Rick's become a person I don't know anymore. He relies
on his manager, whom I find deceitful and manipulative,
for his every need.

Gunnar and Matthew innocently tell me that their
father's girlfriend moved in the day I moved out . . .
girlfriend?

> **T**hey say those were the glory years
> The ones I spent with you
> But life is strange,
> You see—I've changed
> Reality's filtered through

July, 1981

Where'd everybody go? My family? My friends? The kids
will be back from camp next month. Tracy's leaving for
college at the beginning of September.

No ability to concentrate—no energy—no paintings.
Scared of everything.

August, 1981

I met Gus a year ago when I saw him in *Cyrano de
Bergerac*. We've become more than friends during this
summer of overwhelming emptiness. Thank God for his
voice of reason in all this insanity. I can depend on him
and trust him. He's suggested I try painting again, but
in a corner of his apartment this time, where I feel safe.

I remember the color of the jacaranda trees on his street.

"FLUTTERBYE"
KRISTIN NELSON
5-25-81

Butterfly
blinding color dusting
the leather of the mustang

I hold my breath
you watch the night
suddenly it is not so dark

FLUTTERBYE

1981

FOURTH OF JULY ON
CARMELINA AVENUE

1981

August, 1981

An old memory begins to form—the annual Fourth of July parade in the neighborhood.

When we lived in the Carmelina house, there was a tradition of neighbors' gathering on our front lawn every July 4th for lemonade and gossip before the parade began. We created patriotic costumes out of the reds, whites, and blues in our wardrobes. We carried American flags, balloons, banners. One year I made a caterpillar train out of cardboard boxes for the littlest kids. My brother was the caboose.

"Think . . . of the world you carry within you, and call this thinking what you will; whether it be remembering your own childhood or yearning toward your own future. . . ."
Rainer Maria Rilke

August, 1981   New York
We *visited Gus's sister in her Village apartment before going to visit the rest of his family at the Jersey Shore.   New York City is warm, loud, and sparkling tonight.   Everyone here is asleep.*

CRABBING

1981

August, 1981 Jersey Shore

Gus's niece, Pia, is a fearless crabber. She shows seven-year-old Sam—who's game to try anything—how to catch, clean, and cook the crabs in garlic, butter, olive oil, salt, and pepper. Sam seems to be having a great summer. It's nice to be with family again.

I heard Sam screaming down by the dock. I found him standing on the pilings with a fierce hold on his crab trap. If he released his grip, the sides would collapse—and he wasn't going to risk it. His eyes were wild as he examined the monster from the deep that he'd pulled up from below.

My young son had never seen a blowfish before and the one in his trap was furiously puffed up in spiny glory.

JERSEY SHORE

1981

Gunnar and Matt,
summer 1981

August, 1981
Every summer, the older
children have been able to
attend a session or two at
Mountain Meadow Ranch in
northern California. They
really love it there, and
this year Tracy is a junior
counselor. Gus and I drove
the boys' drums up to them
last week, as they requested,
so they could practice with
"their band."

We ask
awestruck
How could the night be so warm?
I discovered
on a windy night
without electricity
that darkness was friendly
not nearly as black as it seemed
I went to sleep with the windows open
Just to be closer to the sky

Tracy Nelson

SUMMER CAMP

1981

September, 1981

Adjusting slowly. Remembering to breathe. I received a painting commission just in time for the holidays. We'll be able to have a nice Christmas.

October, 1981

My father came over tonight and asked to see the progress I'd made on the commission. "What's happened to your colors?" he asked. "Everything's so dark . . ."

December, 1981

Standing in court together—attorneys, instead of each other, at our sides— Rick and I are divorced. He had no visible reaction.

*Close the door—left
right   red door
                    so sad I
grab   myself
hold my hands to
                    my face
confused I
reach for you
    but you're not there
anymore
I said too much
I wanted you to think
            I didn't
care
I
hear you walk away I
know
you have to go I'm
sad I
said too much*

March, 1982

How does one recover from a long illusion? It's always been hard to separate myth from fact.

November, 1982

I drove by the Studio City farmhouse today. It's been three years since we left. Limestone walls have replaced the white corral fences. Best friends' children don't play with mine anymore. The beautiful old oaks have been cut down and replaced with manicured cypress. "It's been extensively remodeled," says the workman as he chips away at the antique tiles and my long-ago dream.

Some things passed in the settlement;
Some things slipped away. Enough's left
That I come back sometimes. The theft
And vandalism were our own.
Maybe we should have known.

W. D. Snodgrass

Life
in
slow
motion.

STUDIO DOOR
1996

6/25/83

Dear Mom—

ever since I can remember I've been writing you love letters. When I was four I taped a note on your pillow that said I LOVE MAMA with a big heart around it. This birthday wish from me is something remarkably similar to those illegible scraps of paper you used to find in strategic places like your mirror or closet door.

~~I would~~ just want you to know how much I love you. There is a unique and sometimes difficult bond between a mother and a daughter— so much of ourselves in each other. You are more important to me than anyone else who has ever passed through my life. If this →

sounds at all silly, I hope you excuse me but it's coming from a very uncomplicated place – after all a child's love letter is never false. You are amazing – intelligent – humorous – powerfully artistic – "a major creative force." So I, and the little girl I used to be, wish you a happy birthday, and give you something frivolous and pretty because WE LOVE MAMA, forever and always.

XO Tracy

March, 1983
Sometimes—at odd times—
there are moments
of real clarity—
but most of the time—
I can't do anything at all.

January, 1984

The manager called to say Rick can't afford to keep the children in private school. The boys have to be taken out in the middle of the school year and Tracy has to leave college.

The boys and I are moving to a little house closer to the ocean. The public school nearby has a good reputation.

Tracy came back to town and landed her first acting interview. She'll be able to support herself, as an actress, when she starts filming a series in a few weeks.

Raised by the women
Who were stronger than you know
A patchwork quilt of memories
Only women could have sewn
Threads were stitched by family hands
Protected from the moth
By her mother, and her mother
The weavers of the cloth
                    Mary Chapin Carpenter

December, 1984

Illusions long since scattered
I let you go.
but every winter
I remember how

you loved Christmas

THE KIDS AT HOME

March, 1985
Unused heart
crated up and stored away
lost inside the person I thought they wanted me to be
for so long
I've felt nothing

August, 1985
My father had an aortic aneurysm. He's undergone
emergency surgery and is in intensive care. I'm all assur-
ance and optimism while waiting with the family at the
hospital. The fluorescent lights cause a greenish haze to
filter through the corridors and we speak in whispers.
Each of us does our part: my sister calls for a priest, my
mother applies lipstick, I bargain with God—if I can
have my father a little longer, I won't take another drink.

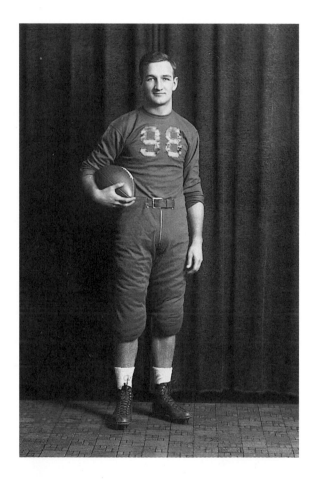

Crumpled bits of paper
Filled with imperfect thought
Stilted conversations
I'm afraid that's all we've got.

You say you just don't see it
He says it's perfect sense
You just can't get agreement
In this present tense
We all talk a different language
Talking in defense.

Say it loud, say it clear
You can listen as well as you hear
It's too late when we die
To admit we don't see eye to eye.
           B A Robertson / Mike Rutherford

THE ATHLETE

THE ATHLETE
© KRISTIN NELSON TINKER
1993

August, 1985

My father's still in intensive care and very weak, but he's going to be all right. There are tubes everywhere.

"Hi, McGill," he says. When he calls my nickname, all's right with the world.

"Hi, Pop." His finger writes phantom letters on the bedsheet: I . . . R . . . I . . . S . . . H. "Irish?"

He smiles and makes the OK sign.

September, 1985

At least casting forces some sort of human contact. I know I must be around people right now—it would be all too easy to become a hermit. I'm not sure where I go from here—living from day to day is so stressful but even if I had the time or energy to paint, I couldn't bring in enough to support all of us—I need my day job to get by.

October, 1985 Indiana

My father's home recovering. I'm casting a movie in the Midwest, where he was born—working with young athletes on a film called Hoosiers. Observing these kids in the movie,

I understand my father better.

Sports are a way of life in Indiana.

Harvest time
a simpler life
fall in the air
sorghum.
hand-painted ads
weathered barns
along the two-lane.
frozen vegetables
chicken-fried steak
long hours
and a tiny feeling
of accomplishment

October, 1985

One changes when the heart is involved
—my father's old fight is gone—he's
more distant and withdrawn. I assure
him he's on his way to a full recovery
because it occurs to me he thinks we're
withholding bad news—such is my
family's way of dealing with unpleasant
information.

There's a greatness about him—
something that makes me want to
please him. Although he's an enigma to
me and his compliments come through
sarcasm and criticism and he's loud—
quiet—sensitive—shy—tough—abrupt
—competitive and kind—I understand
him. There's no one that I love more.

Matt and Gunnar—eighteen last
month—want to move out—"to get to
know Pop." I hold my breath and let
them go.

November, 1985

In the casting office
the Man from Milwaukee
introduced himself
lowered his glasses
and smiled at me
with eyes that had the effect
of a closed door

Mick said
the cute one wants to ask you out.

We had
dinner by the sea
talked
laughed
shared our dreams
each other

orchids
phone calls
letters followed
and a month later
we went to Santa Fe
with no expectations

expecting a little

by candlelight
and snow on the window
he looked at photographs
of my paintings

early in the morning
dawn broke in
violet directions
and we remembered
distant melodies
and infinite possibility

dust covered
from a long time ago

November, 1985

The Man from Milwaukee's
a seductive poet
loving letters from the Midwest.
". . . chili lights . . . pumpkin soup . . .
barbecued turkey in the snow . . .
thinking of you . . . missing you . . ."
signed with an

MARCY STREET CARD SHOP, SANTA FE

1985

November, 1985 Thanksgiving
Paper turkeys hang from clothespins
drying in the classroom window at
Sam's school. The children play outdoors
in shirtsleeves, but winter is in the air—
or at least I pretend a change of seasons
every evening with the setting sun.

December, 1985
My mother and father have helped me
convert the garage into a studio. We cut
a small door into the west wall for
access into the house. An old window
from the Santa Monica Pier was
installed for light.

Rain, creeping
in from the sea as it did
thoughtful   introspective days
days to paint
write   introspective days
to think about a new flavor of coffee bean
listening to classical music days

Inexplicable anxiety
*   Rick consciously choosing to become*
a parody of himself—
*   He's "Ricky" again—the unhealthiest*
of all choices.

December 31, 1985 New Year's Eve
The manager has proved to be a lethal choice.
After years of his threats and my reporting him
to the police, I knew he would never be
calling me   —unless—
—it was his voice on the answering machine—
"Kris . . ."   he said . . . "call me back right
away . . .   there's been . . .   an . . .
*   um . . .   accident with the plane . . .*
*   it . . .   ah . . .   it doesn't look like*
Rick made it . . ."
Here it comes—
*   the falling apart—*
*   the black spaces—*

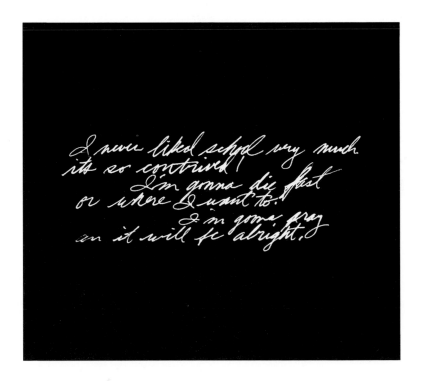

From
Rick's journal

I remember a time back when
Papa would laugh as I held his hand
And just one embrace would make my troubles pass

I thought those days would never end
The day that he left he smiled and he said,
"I'll be home soon"—but Papa never came back

                            I hear him saying

Love me today—let my strength be your own
Love me today—because tomorrow I'll be gone
When I feel it's time to go, I'll be on my way
So love me today.

Don't be afraid to say, "I love you."
Take the moment and make it last
'Cause if you don't tell me you love me
You might not get a second chance

                            So hear me saying

Love me today—let my strength be your own
Love me today—because tomorrow I'll be gone
When I feel it's time to go, I'll be on my way
So love me today.

             Gunnar Nelson and Matthew Nelson

May, 1986

Surreal days and months. Rick leaves
behind the saddest legacy of all—he'll
never know his children and they'll
never know their father. And now, he is
canonized because of an untimely death.

Gone, I say and walk from the church,
refusing the stiff procession to the grave,
letting the dead ride alone in the hearse.
It is June. I am tired of being brave.
                         Anne Sexton

July, 1986

With time, I hope I'll be less angry.

There are people in your life who've
      come and gone
They let you down and hurt your pride
Better put it all behind you; life goes on
You keep carryin' that anger, it'll eat
      you up inside
               Don Henley / Mike Campbell /
                      John David Souther

August, 1986 Chicago

Life's a game of pick-up-sticks since he died. I'm in Chicago with the Man from Milwaukee for a little while. There's nothing more seductive, or distracting, than a long-distance relationship. His apartment is all music and light. We watch the world from the sixteenth floor —sleep in a sunny corner—have dinner by candlelight and James Taylor sings "Song for You" in the background. I do pen-and-ink drawings of the city while he works during the day. We talk about living together when he moves to California in early winter and about driving across the country and stopping in Santa Fe on the way to the Coast.

> *And love grew in the garden
> rested in sunny rooms
> was quiet
> in the early morning
> and filled the world with laughter*
>
> *Holding you
> I'm aware
> of the loneliness
> we share
> after not quite a year
> standing there*

December, 1986

Our first Christmas together—Sam and me and the Man from Milwaukee in the little house by the ocean. His children visit for the holidays. Sushi and a gold-and-diamond band for New Year's.

February, 1987

All is not well. I suspect the Milwaukee Man has other interests at his new job. He tells me I'm imagining things. The headaches and the black spaces are back. I have a feeling as if in a nightmare—of this all being something repeated—something I've already been through—and have to go through all over again.

> *April, 1987*
>
> *Without inspiration
> instincts gone—self-destructive
> long time coming—
> indiscreet breakdown*

May, 1987

He's gone—an intense and strangely distant memory. We shared a passionate suspension in time and now it's over.

Desolation—despair—life without meaning—compressed—crazed— empty—numb—nothing. Still, I do not drink and don't understand why pills won't cure a heart more broken.

> For the thing which I greatly feared is come upon me, and that which I was afraid of is come unto me.
>
> It was not in safety, neither had I rest, neither was I quiet; yet trouble came.
> Job 3:25–26

May, 1987

*I can't seem to work my way out of this.
I need help. My brother has generously
offered to pay for a month's stay in rehab
for me. He's also promised to take care
of Sam until I return home. All he wants,
he says, is for me to get well.*

May, 1987 The Hospital

*Checking in, I feel like some sort of
criminal. My brother stands by and
watches closely. He doesn't understand
—that I understand—I need to do
this. As hard as this will be, I welcome
these thirty days. Mumbling something
to me about "tough love"—he leaves.*

May, 1987

*Sudden apprehension and anxiety.
But he's trying to help me.
I want to leave—I—
must leave right away.*

*I asked Gus to pick me up and went
to his place. I slept for two days.*

May, 1987 The Hospital, again.

*Thinking more clearly, I checked in
again, on my own. I have a month to
become honest with myself—time to get
well and understand what's happened.*

May, 1987 The Hospital

*My brother's making everything so
difficult. He doesn't bring my son to
visit me. He refuses to attend family
counseling sessions and has denied
Sam the opportunity to share in my
recovery as well. He just doesn't seem
to understand the recovery process
and refuses to learn. He's always been
determined to do things his way.*

142

June, 1987 The Hospital

*Every little thought from the outside
world is intensified a thousand times.
This is the toughest thing I've ever done.*

*June, 1987
Family Counseling Session*

"Why are you so angry?
You weren't angry as a child."

June, 1987 The Hospital
For My Mother

*I'm beginning to realize
I shattered the illusion
of your perfect family*

*I know you worked hard
and I understand
your fierce determination
to make everything beautiful*

*It's just that
I needed the truth*

*I didn't want to die
just to kill
the death in me
and failing that*

I wanted to feel nothing

June, 1987 The Hospital

Children with injuries can come out of any kind of family. Secret things are handed down, generation after generation. The entire family suffers from an inability to communicate honestly with one another. Our roles have been assigned in an unspoken consensus of opinion by all family members. My sister has been labeled the peacemaker, while my brother thrives in his role of rescuer. I've been the designated problem ever since I can remember. I am the sick one, they remind me. If they fix me, then they'll be fine.

At the family therapy sessions everyone has their own agenda. There are too many of them and too few counselors.

Five minutes before visiting hours are over, the Man from Milwaukee walks into my hospital room unannounced. His hair is blown dry—bigger than I remember—and he has a sunburn. He says that his visit shouldn't be misinterpreted—in fact, he says quickly, he's seeing others. There's a sudden rash on my neck and I'm hot all over—but I don't run away and I don't feel like dying. Who is this other person I find getting well?

Dark outside—stars through hermetically sealed windows. I'll be discharged tomorrow. Is there anything left for me?

June, 1987 The Hospital

My brother's been busy while I've been in the hospital. I was handed a summons this morning as I was checking out. Through his attorney, he says he wants permanent custody of my youngest son. I have to find a lawyer and get to court by this afternoon.

June, 1987

And in all of this, Tracy's announced her engagement. She plans to marry William Remington Moses July 25th on Catalina Island.

July, 1987

I've never known my brother's dark side. It's possible that I've never really known him. Trying to balance between prewedding festivities and the process servers who attempt to subpoena me, and my children to testify against me.

What I do know is that he's picked a bad time to do all this. I am well and stronger than I've been in a very long time.

And slowly life begins.

July, 1987 Catalina Island

Garden roses, pastels, violins, and a wedding at sunset. Tracy and Billy look like porcelain dolls—all youth and hope. Sam gives his sister away, and Gunnar and Matthew accompany me to a seat next to Harriet. On a hillside overlooking the ocean, a white cross wrapped in a wreath of gardenias stands in Rick's memory.

"Hope" is the thing with feathers—
That perches in the soul—
And sings the tune without the words—
And never stops—at all—

Emily Dickinson

UPON A STAR

1989

August, 1987
Superior Court of California, City of Los Angeles

In all his single-mindedness, my brother has no idea of the irreparable damage he is doing to an already fragile family. We're due in court this morning. I've heard that my new sister-in-law, who I've met only briefly, is telling the people she works with that she's adopting a twelve-year-old boy. Is she speaking about my son?

Today with no makeup, circle pin and great authority, the same sister-in-law testifies she would make a better mother to my son. My brother—who communicates with me through attorneys only—sits with my parents and my sister and her children. The judge has allowed Sam to sit in on the proceedings. My twelve-year-old, with his baseball cap pulled low on his forehead so I can't see his eyes, listens stone-faced as his new aunt describes herself as more fitting to be his mother. My three older children refuse to support their uncle, so he refuses to talk to them. I sit with old and dear friends—Susan and Gus.

After years of paranoia and uncertainty, I suppose there's something freeing about seeing one's perceived enemies all lined up in a single bench on the opposite side of the courtroom.

And the people all said sit down
Sit down
Sit down, you're rockin' the boat
Frank Loesser

August, 1987

It's the third day of the trial and my attorney has a chance to cross-examine my brother's wife. He is smiling this Monday morning. "Your brother wants to call it quits," he tells me. "He doesn't want his wife's past to be scrutinized in public." And just like that, it's over. The judge reprimands my brother for wasting the court's time. My son is coming home. My brother doesn't make eye contact.

The courthouse is crowded with press. Because I am embarrassed for Mark, I take his hand as we walk past the crowd. Later that day, Sam and his possessions are unceremoniously left at my front door.

I don't need you to worry for me cause I'm alright
I don't want you to tell me it's time to come home
I don't care what you say anymore, this is my life
Go ahead with your own life and leave me alone
Billy Joel

FAMILY REUNION

1992

MARK IS BACK
IN TOWN

1987

September, 1987
When the custody battle began, I called Mark Tinker—my brother's producer, director, and good friend, of the TV show St. Elsewhere, *to solicit a little help in talking to my brother. Surely my brother would listen to a man like Mark before going public with his custody fight.*

November, 1987
Tracy is very sick. She noticed the glands on her neck were swollen and has been having night sweats. The doctors are doing tests.

December, 1987
I sit in Tracy's hospital room before they take her down to surgery. My mother and father are here, too, but they don't speak to me. My daughter is so ill and I'm very scared, but there are no words of comfort. In their eyes, I've disgraced the family.

December, 1987
Christmas Eve
So still in the hospital. Tracy's sleeping lightly—it's very late and everyone's gone home; the two of us are alone on Christmas Eve. Her room's illuminated by the little bubble lights on the tree in the corner. Carols play softly in the background.

His voice is like a string of richly colored beads

Although my brother remained inflexible and bullheaded, Mark Tinker was supportive. After each day in court he called to talk to me—giving me a perspective on the public proceedings and the evening news reports.

I *especially like it when he says, "Hi—it's Mark."*

My beautiful daughter has been married less than six months. Her symptoms have been confirmed and the diagnosis is Hodgkin's lymphoma—cancer of the lymph glands. She's elected to have radical treatment—removal of her spleen and months of chemotherapy and radiation—because with it, her prognosis is excellent.

Tracy's operation went well, but it is extremely difficult to see one's child suffering so. Billy's been very considerate—inviting me along when he visits her in intensive care. The long recovery begins slowly.

My friend Mark has been a great comfort to me. We've talked every day in these last months and shared a deep and exhilarating connection. He's a very special person. I really care about him. I thought maybe he'd like a small painting for Christmas. He wants to move back east someday. There's a picture of his Connecticut dream house tacked up in the kitchen.

I finish hanging the antique glass beads she loves and kiss her sleeping forehead as I leave.

"Merry Christmas, Mom," she says. "I love you."

"Merry Christmas, Trace. I love you, too."

When the elevator door opens, Mark Tinker is standing there.

"Merry Christmas," he says. "You look like you could use a friend."

149

CHAPTER FIVE

1988–1991

SAFE AT HOME

1993

January, 1988

*I'd heard
about Mark Tinker
for years, but we didn't actually meet until early last summer when we ended up as teammates in a
softball game and said hello like old friends. We
continued talking at a barbecue after the game. I noticed
his David Letterman T-shirt and he took it off and gave it to me—
continuing the conversation half naked with a noticeably attractive body
and a twinkle in his eye. 
Coming as I did from a background of double meanings,
Mark's uncanny honesty and total directness were going to take some
getting used to—he didn't have any censors attached. I was just getting
up to speed and he was full-speed ahead, saying exactly what was on
his mind, telling the truth directly, never looking back. We ran on
different clocks—we were worlds apart—but I recog-
nized a kindred spirit and I liked him enormously.
Sometime after that first meeting, roses arrived with a card. He made me smile. I
knew then that sometime in the
future we might be
more than good
friends.*

Kris—

First you like
my shirt — then my
sweatshirt... If
you tell me you
like Jockey shorts
I know I'm in
trouble.

Love,
Mark

February, 1988

Once upon a time, in a faraway land, there was a princess who was kept locked up by her family in a very high tower. She was closed in that room all day and she couldn't talk to anyone. One day, a mouse appeared in her room.

"Hello," he said. "I am a magical mouse. I am here to grant your every wish!"

The princess thought the mouse was cool, but she was pretty skeptical. She didn't trust anybody. Not even a mouse.

With a little time, patience, love, and understanding, the princess and the mouse became friends. As soon as he thought it wouldn't scare her, the mouse turned into a semi-intelligent, somewhat balding, extremely nice male being. The princess liked him and even began to trust him a little.

The mouse made promises he said he could keep—all the princess had to do was believe him. Most important of all, the mouse promised to take care of the princess always and let no harm come to her.

And so the princess and the magical mouse lived forever in a beautiful home by the sea. And they were happy all day long, and they listened to music, and made love, and loved each other forevermore.

Fairy tale: MCT to KHN

February, 1988

After I cooked dinner for him at my house, Mark slapped his hands down hard on the table (making the candles flicker and the dogs and me jump) and declared, "This is the way it's supposed to be!" Last night, he asked me to marry him.

April 20, 1988

Mark and I were married in the backyard of our home by the sea. Silk ribbons on our wedding tree rippled in the wind during the sunset ceremony, and at dusk luminaries lit the garden. My daughter, finished with her radiation and chemotherapy treatments, was able to be my matron of honor. Mark's son, eight-year-old Jake, was best man. The violinists played "Wouldn't It Be Nice" and it really was.

But holding you close is like holding the summer sun
I'm warm from the memory of days to come

Billy Joel

May, 1988

Mark asked me, "What is it you want to do? What is at the top of your list?" and I answered—"To paint."
I'd never said it out loud.
And I see it in his eyes—showing me what love is supposed to look like.

"You can do anything you want to do. What is rare is this actual wanting to do a specific thing: wanting it so much that you are blind to all other things, that nothing else will satisfy you . . .

". . . There is reason for you to give this statement some of your best thought. You may find that this is just what's the matter with most of the people of the world; that few are really wanting what they think they want, and that most people go through their lives without doing one whole thing they really want to do . . ."

Robert Henri

To paint what love is

April 14, 1988

Dear Mom—

I can't tell you how honoured I am to "stand up for you". This
is a wonderful life affirming occasion that makes me feel
closer to you than ever before. I am so happy for you — both
of you are very very lucky. If I could make one wedding wish
came true for you it would be that you treasure what you have
forever — because it just gets better & better.
        I love you very very much — Happy wedding — Trace xxx

AND THEN WE'LL BE HAPPY

1988

155

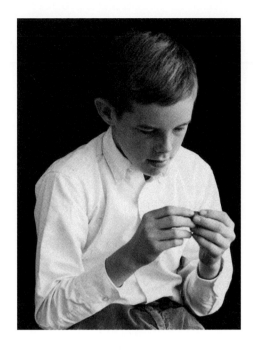

"I thought
if we drove
fast enough,
we could go
between
the raindrops…"

Mark, age eight

I'm in a hurry to get things done
Oh I rush and rush until life's no fun
All I really gotta do is live and die
But I'm in a rush and don't know why
Randy Van Warmer / Roger Murrah

June, 1988
W*e discovered the Vineyard
on a rented motor scooter.
When it broke down, Mark,
admittedly no mechanic,
became frustrated, then
angry, and walked away.
Upset by his impatience,
I took his cue—and walked
in the opposite direction.
But life is too short; I turned
around almost immediately
and met him halfway.*

Oh—and she never gives out
And she never gives in
She just changes her mind
Billy Joel

August, 1988
M*ark received his twelfth
Emmy nomination and
last night, when he won his
Emmy, I was by his side.
He said I brought him luck.
In his acceptance speech, he
thanked everyone he worked
with, his son, the kids, and
me—his new family.*

September, 1988
W*e moved into a temporary
house in the Pacific Palisades.
It's like a fraternity living
with all our boys—Gunnar,
Matthew, Sam, and Jake—
at home. Tracy and Billy
live close by—just down the
canyon. My family is whole
again.*

My children dance and dream...

February, 1989

Too much time spent being the mother and wife I was supposed to be and the person I had to be in order to survive. I don't feel guilty about being me anymore— I feel curiously free.

My husband has made it possible for Sam to finish his last two years of high school in the East. After skating on asphalt all summer, Sam's a good enough ice skater to make his school's hockey team—a dream come true for him. He's come through these last years intact and is moving ahead—determined to get an education.

Gunnar and Matthew are touring with their band and doing very well after signing their first record deal. Their postcard reads: "Hi folks! Australia Rocks!"

Tracy's been working steadily since she started acting—alternating between TV and film roles. She's a wonderful actress with a real gift for comedy.

Jake is happy in school. He likes to draw and is doing very well.

I'm so proud of all the kids—individuals all— independent—creative— articulate—courageous and funny.

April, 1989

Our dream house—a two-story, blue-shingled cape— sits on top of Santa Monica Canyon overlooking the Pacific Ocean. We'll be moving in by our first anniversary.

Mark promises to build a studio over the garage one day—but until then, he encourages me to rent a space close by where I can paint. The magical mouse has integrity. He's taking care of me.

Here a star, and there a star,
Some lose their way!
Here a mist, and there a mist,
Afterwards—Day!

Emily Dickinson

June, 1989

I turned forty-four on Sunday and had lunch with my family—with my parents, too. The hurt runs deep, but I want to be friends with them again. I've accepted the blame for all the trouble and I've apologized. It wasn't difficult to say I'm sorry.

Just, it's time to get on with it. Even if they don't want to believe me—I know I'm okay.

My parents are still tentative—suspicious— it gets complicated when the family problem isn't a problem anymore.

...history

Sifts down through the glass like snow, and we
Wonder if her single deed tells much
Or little of the way she loves, and whether he
Sees shadows in the sky . . .

Gjertrud Schnackenberg

158

"SUPPOSING IT SNOWED"
KRATH-NEVEON TINKER
11-3-89

SUPPOSING IT SNOWED

1989

June, 1989

In Santa Monica Canyon, just down the hill from our house, I found a converted garage that's for rent, month to month—a perfect painting place. The chili lights went up yesterday. Now I have the time to paint and a commitment to myself and ideas filed away for years.

Mark is tough, stimulating. With him, I am never bored. I love the way he electrifies a room with his presence. Although we're a match of opposites, there are many lessons to be learned from each other.

A few nice commissions have come my way.

BOCA DE BACA

1989

HEART OF THE MANOR

1990

THE VACANT LOT
1954
KRISTIN NELSON TINKER
7-14-89

162

Now you look down. The waters of childhood are there.
Mark Strand

July, 1989

My tree grew in the vacant lot across the street from the house on Sunswept Drive.

The large California pepper was my *sanctuary* from the rest of the world.

Childhood fantasies were sheltered under the safe haven of branches and leaves

and I *imagined* there with all ten-year-old *possibility.*

In spring foxtails and wildflowers covered the hillside in shades of green and violet, and the meadow

came alive with spotted ladybugs, skippers, and cabbage butterflies.

"**O**ne brush stroke and an hour has passed. How can I explain what's happened?"
Georgia O'Keeffe

THE VACANT LOT
1989

September, 1989

My girlfriend Annabella recently purchased her dream
home—a yellow adobe above the tiny town of Galisteo,
just south of Santa Fe. Because I received a profit when
I sold the little house that my father helped me purchase,
I have enough to invest in a small second home. The
old, one-engine Galisteo fire station has been converted
into a living space and put up for sale. It sounds perfect!

October, 1989

A cold winter wind swept over the plains, over the village,
and over Annabella and me as we sought shelter on the
steps of the small church. We ate a takeout lunch as we
waited for our friend and realtor, Chris, who was driving
down from Santa Fe to show us the fire station.

There is no vista as breathtakingly beautiful as the
approach to Galisteo. The little town sits in the center of
the vast plains—one of the oldest settlements in the South-
west. Surrounded by ancient ridgeback mountains that
are covered with petroglyphs, the center of town consists
of the Catholic church and Anaya's one-room general
store. Hot coffee and homemade burritos are the house
specialty—especially welcome this day.

Halfway down the road with no name and just east
of Highway 41—and close to my friend—is the old fire
station. The building has been enclosed by an adobe wall
and lovingly converted into a residence.

There is a huge garden—inspiring even in winter,
with every variety of fruit tree. The old gnarled peach
tree outside the kitchen window is rumored to have been
planted by Father Lamy, the first archbishop of New Mexico.

"Heaven"—is what I cannot reach!
The Apple on the Tree—
Provided it do hopeless—hang—
That—"Heaven" is—to Me!

The Color, on the Cruising Cloud—
The interdicted Land—
Behind the Hill—The House behind—
There—Paradise—is found!

Emily Dickinson

The wonderful house comes with an orange
cat—an independent and hearty soul named
Murphy. He greets us with his half-tail held high.

THE CAT WHO CAME
WITH THE HOUSE

1991

November, 1989 Galisteo

Mark hasn't seen Galisteo or the firehouse yet, so we decided to fly from Los Angeles to Albuquerque and drive in on the back road. After years of wishing and hoping, it's hard to believe this house—in my favorite place on earth—is ours.

I'd like to think I stayed in LA my whole life just to make sense of it—but in my heart I know I lacked the courage to move on.

We turned off the highway where it intersects with the church—past the cottonwoods that line the river. Dirt roads wind through the village before the Galisteo bridge.

Stacked rocks divide property lines, as they have for centuries. A llama peeked over a wall, her coat heavy with winter. As we rounded the corner, an adobe wall opened at the wooden gate to Murphy in the winter sun.

A very special Thanksgiving—the first snow of the season this morning, the smell of piñon wood in the fireplace and the aroma of fresh herbs as the turkey cooked in the afternoon. Murphy now has his own cat door so he can come out of the weather. He's been dubbed "the mayor" by Joe and Debbie, our next-door neighbors.

November, 1989
Los Angeles

Memory paintings come with more frequency—something to do with new health and self-confidence.

Halloween. My mother made our costumes. I was a leprechaun one year— in green sequins and tights. Up the street the lady in the two-story house threw dimes from her upstairs window instead of giving candy at the front door.

January, 1990

The Palisades by the Santa Monica Pier were a natural grandstand to watch the local fireworks on the Fourth of July. We'd pack a picnic basket and plenty of blankets and arrive early to reserve our spot on the cliff.

KID NIGHT

1990

FREEDOM ROCK
(Before the Curfew)

1990

The last picture of my father with the family, 1990
(from left to right, bottom row: Grace [the boys' dog], Sam and Matthew
Nelson, Jake Tinker, Gunnar Nelson, Kris Nelson Tinker, Tracy Nelson, Kelly
Harmon Miller and her two daughters, Samantha and Elissa Miller. Top row: my
father, Tom Harmon, Mark Tinker, and my mother, Elyse Knox Harmon.)

February, 1990

I stopped by my parents' house this evening. My father was watching TV in his den. The volume was turned up loud, I had to yell hello. He seemed glad to see me, but was listless and pale. Most disconcerting of all was the faraway look in his eyes.

March 15, 1990

This morning, as Mark was leaving for work, he said, "Beware the Ides of March."

I worked in my studio all day and just before dark completed a window painting—actually a set of windows that were curved at the top—with the Galisteo church, a STOP sign, and black clouds painted overhead. I thought the black clouds curious. Then, by no means a pressing matter, I picked up the phone to confirm some travel reservations for Sam. My travel agent is also a friend, so I was pleasantly surprised when she picked up her office phone after business hours.

"Hi, it's Kris," I said.

She sounded out of breath. "Kris?"

Before I could answer, she put me on hold.

She clicked back some time later. "Where are you?"

"At my studio," I said.

"Thank God you called," she said. "Your father was just here and said he wasn't feeling well; then he collapsed in my office. He's been taken to UCLA cardiac emergency."

"I'm on my way," I said.

Then, as gently as she could, my friend added, "It doesn't look good."

I called Mark at work. Somehow he arrived at the emergency room before I did and was waiting when I walked in. We found ourselves in a room with my brother and his wife. We hadn't spoken in almost three years. Nobody knew how to find my mother or sister.

The doctor came into the room and spoke to the four of us with a cheery smile. He said that my father had had a heart attack and went on to explain all the procedures that had been taken to save his life. And then he added . . . "But we couldn't save him."

Pardon me? No. Impossible.

My husband put his arms around me. It had been five years since my father's aneurysm. I'd bargained with God for more time and he'd given it to me. I'd kept my promise, too.

NO

March, 1990

I know my mother and father truly loved each other. I don't know how my mother felt either before or after my father died, because we don't talk about feelings.

These days of loss
  still uncounted
  still unknown
trying to fill
the empty places
that he took with him
    Edward George Garren

March, 1990

*H**is den. His room. His desk. His things. The swivel chair he sat in to communicate with the world. The aroma of his pipe still lingers—I can hear the sound of his fingers on the typewriter.*

When I was a little kid, my father's desk was a treasure chest of magical items: pen—paper—scissors—glue—tape—a paper cutter—carbon paper—staples—paper clips. He had a place for everything.

I escaped into books from his library—the beginning of my self-education, which consisted of novels of espionage and adventure and true-life stories from World War II. Reading wasn't just a way to pass the time—it was the start of my lifelong passion to learn more. It was easy to become the people and events in these books. They gave me permission to believe in possibility.

Wedged between others, a small book caught my eye. I don't remember the exact title. It had to do with Irish legend and I opened to a page that read . . .

When an Irishman dies
it is believed
his soul flies free
in the form of a white butterfly

I have been comforted ever since by the frequent sightings of white butterflies. I believe they're my father's way of checking in—just saying hi.

Old 98: Harmon Was Someone Special to the End

Jim Murray

THE DAY HE DIED
1990

April, 1990

I've looked for that little book ever since I replaced it on the shelf and it's nowhere to be found. Was it there that day because I needed comfort? I did find a letter in his desk which was addressed to me the preceding August and never sent.

171

April, 1990

I *had* the dream again *last night.*

My childhood home on Sunswept Drive

had low ceilings and dark hallways

that led downstairs through my parents' bedroom,

past **my father's desk** *to the Dutch door.*

I was standing outside, under an overhang on the back patio that was also my **backyard theater.**

The neighborhood assembled to watch the play. I was wearing the Cinderella dress

my mother had sewn at midnight and

I asked my father to light the magic wand.

As I walked in back of the circular wall, it fell apart.

I was looking for something I'd left behind.

I wanted to find what was missing.

See the two dogs burst into sight. When you leave,
they will cease, snuffed out in the glare of an earlier light.
Visit the neighbors down the block; he waters his lawn,
she sits on her porch, but not for long.
When you look again they're gone.

Keep going back, back to the field, flat and sealed in mist.
On the other side, a man and woman are waiting;
they have come back, your mother before she was gray,
your father before he was white.

Mark Strand

May, 1990

My brother and I were brought together by the death of our father, so Mark and I accepted my brother's Easter invitation to come with our children to an egg hunt at his house. He and his wife also invited my sister and her family, my mother, and Harriet. Mark and Jake dressed as an Easter Bunny and Easter Chicken and distributed dyed eggs to the little ones.

I've painted
family members twice,
wondering,
Was it real?

GOOD EGGS

1990

my backyard - galisteo summer 1990

R. Murphy

June, 1990

Galisteo

spring escapes into summer. The wild New Mexican daisies intermingle with the last of spring's red poppies. Leaves on the twisted willow are a new shade of green and the cottonwoods shadow the beginnings of the hollyhocks. Murphy guards the hammock strung between the trees.

All is well.

MY BACKYARD
GALISTEO, SUMMER

1990

APODOCA HILL

1987

LITTLE WHITE CLOUD (APODOCA HILL 2)

1987

Our isolated little world of light,

Covered with snow, and snow clouds above it,
And drifts and swirls too deep to understand.
Still, I must try to think a little of it,
With so much winter in my head and hand.
Gjertrud Schnackenberg

BACKROAD
1991

August, 1990

There was peace for a little while, then my brother hired yet another attorney, signaling the end of the truce. Now he wants to take over as Sam's trustee. After another round of legal machinations and attorney fees, the court rules that my brother has no say in my son's affairs. I don't understand his animosity; I only understand this has become a control issue for him and it's time to walk away.

My brother, man, if you would know the truth,
We both are by the same dull walls shut in;
The gate is massive and the dungeon strong.
But you look through the key-hole out beyond,
And call this knowledge; yet have not at hand
The key wherein to turn the fatal lock.
                                        Victor Hugo

I had no time to Hate—
Because
The Grave would hinder Me—
And Life was not so
Ample I
Could finish—Enmity—
                    Emily Dickinson

October, 1990 Galisteo

The aspens turn a brilliant yellow and their leaves shimmer toward earth in the afternoon light. Winter's chill is in the air. Murphy climbs the kiva ladder to the roof and lays next to the solar panels to keep warm.

LAND OF THE FREE

1991

January 16, 1991

My husband's fortieth birthday. His father helps me surprise him with a party which begins at the same time CNN televises the start of the Gulf War.

March, 1991

General Schwarzkopf is my hero. The country celebrates minimal loss of life and yellow ribbons are displayed everywhere. Our men are coming home.

March, 1991
My mother casually mentions that she and my brother
have scattered my father's ashes without telling my sister
and me. I tell myself it doesn't matter, but I'm a wounded
kid all over again and so tired of

the pain game.

The more I know, the less I understand
All the things I thought I knew, I'm learning again
I've been tryin' to get down
    to the heart of the matter
But my will gets weak
    and my thoughts seem to scatter
But I think it's about forgiveness
Forgiveness
Even if, even if you don't love me anymore
    Don Henley / Mike Campbell / John David Souther

I turn it over in my palm
And watch it snowing in another life,
Another world, and from this scene learn what
It is to stand apart
    Gjertrud Schnackenberg

MILES NINE LIVES

1991

May, 1991
A *reverse painting on glass—Tracy and Billy's cat, Miles (full name: Miles from Nowhere), who is a person really—in the form of a cat.*

June, 1991
O *n an old window—my unforgettable and irreplaceable companion, sweet little Rose.*

R *ose is snoring*
dreaming of cats
and chocolate chip cookies

lifting her head
ears alert
she sniffs at the air
imaginary rabbits

she's an old girl now
spends her days
lying in the sun
fat belly up

or scavenging the kitchen
nose to the floor
a cornflake here
a raisin there

she's been my friend
for fourteen years
through the good times
and the bad

always understanding
ever forgiving
I can't imagine her
days being numbered

ROSE ON THE RUG

1991

FAMILY TIES
1991

Dear Kris,

Happy Anniversary

♡

I love you for making my life more wonderful than I thought possible. You are everything to me but we ain't seen nothing yet!

all my love forever,
XXXX OOOO Mark

August, 1991

We attended the summer wedding of Mark's brother Michael to Kathy Mobley. His family and the bride's family have been wonderful to me. Everyone was in attendance.

To wait an Hour—is long—
If Love be just beyond—
To wait Eternity—is short—
If Love reward the end—
                    Emily Dickinson

August, 1991

Mark is keeping the cards and letters coming. After three and a half years he still makes me smile.

November, 1991

My grandmother wasn't educated in the academic sense, but she was the wisest woman I ever knew. She was a wonderful cook. Every meal was a time-consuming work of art. She was generous and kind. Everything she did—she did with her heart. I don't ever remember Nana being still, unless I count the days the Dodgers had a game. But even if she was listening to the kitchen radio, she'd be shelling peas or writing letters to her family in Europe. Her hands were never idle.

She died—*this* was the way she died.
And when her breath was done
Took up her simple wardrobe
And started for the sun.
Her little figure at the gate
The Angels must have spied,
Since I could never find her
Upon the mortal side.

Emily Dickinson

Dec. 6/1976

Dear Cathrine

I am so sorry your Fred has left us. Our deepest Sympathy to you and familie. I know you all must miss him an awful lot but you said he was suffering so much and they could not help him. It was so much better God took him, you see nothing can hurt your Fred anymore. That should be a little Comford to you Cathrine. One day we all have to go.

I be 80 Year old in a Week and counting my days as I am not well, but thanful I lived that long. I have 5 great grand Children.

I am glad Otto is in good healht and your familie too please give them my love.

Best Wishes
for the Hollydays

Nana's letter
to her cousin

NANA
AT THE DOOR

1991

"The conscious of the quest—the realization,
upon reaching this point in life, that this is
what the struggle has been about and that we
can take the rewards forward with us."
Elizabeth Stevenson

December, 1991
Another world. Another time.
A connection to some deep level of consciousness.
A spiritual place on the journey.

Skaters curve
all day across the lake, scoring their white
records in ice.
Howard Nemerov

December, 1991
It's Christmas in New York City. Little
white lights and skaters in Central
Park—blanketed horses—softly falling
snow—the smell of roasted chestnuts

and peace
in my heart.

CHAPTER SIX

1992–1996

TWO PEAS

1992

May, 1992

Now I know why the paintings—which I discounted for so long—were important to me. I didn't understand what compelled me to paint—only that the paintings mattered enormously.

Expressions of intimacy...
lifesavers.

He was weak, and I was strong—then—
So He let me lead him in—
I was weak, and He was strong then—
So I let him lead me—Home.

'Twasn't far—the door was near—
'Twasn't dark—for He went—too
'Twasn't loud, for He said nought—
That was all I cared to know.
                              Emily Dickinson

June, 1992
*Distance
other places*

*a love that's constant and true
a kind heart*

*to value each other
in this time
to cherish life
every day*

Second time for us on Martha's Vineyard. It's so beautiful, so quiet here. This is a time to get to know each other. We share a hope to live back east someday. There are wind chimes and the sound of the ocean outside the old barn where we're spending a summer month. Primitive and elegant, the barn sits on the highest point of land around Squibnocket Pond. The garden grows full of green beans, summer squash, and tomatoes. A dirt road winds through the dunes and sea grass to the ocean, past the back porch, where we spend afternoons reading or watching an occasional squall off the Atlantic.

And through the window from the sleeping loft each dawn, intense shades of violet and vermillion burst into the sky.

June, 1992

*A short ride to the little village of
Menemsha, where we watch the daily
catch being brought in and old boats
secured with half-hitch knots. From
the little walk-up café, we share homemade clam chowder, corn on the cob.
Stars beginning in the sky.*

*In the half-light and quiet of the
evening comes a praying time for me—
a meditation of sorts—where lately,
the word "artist" forms and faintly comes
into focus after my name—glowing
on the horizon with the setting sun—
almost within my grasp.*

A MIDNIGHT CLEAR

1993

ON THE VINEYARD

1991

June, 1992

*Morning in the barn. Mark was shaking
me, waking me. "What're you dreaming about? You're talking in your sleep."
I heard his voice, but I didn't open my
eyes—I wanted to find a resolution to
the dream. It is still with me:*

*We are in the Sunswept house—
my mother and Thirza the seamstress,
and a little girl who intends to speak
her mind.*

*My mother is in her dressing room
with a three-way, floor-length mirror
and a taffeta-covered ottoman.
"Rhapsody in Blue" plays from somewhere. The windows of the room are
covered with a fine film, but the sun
filters through in a narrow stream that
illuminates the figure of my mother.*

*She adjusts the shoulder pads of her
long satin robe. Thirza, with pins in
her mouth, begins the fitting. My mother
tells me it's my turn next and Thirza
giggles, dropping some pins on the floor.*

*Material is wrapped around me
as I stand in front of the mirror. The
room becomes maroon-colored—I can't
breathe. My mother doesn't notice—
she's smiling at me, saying the material
is nice—how pretty I am.*

*I'm trying to tell her what's happen-
ing to me, but no words come—*

*Mark shook me awake. "Kris, you're
yelling. Wake up!"*

"What'd I say?" I asked.

*"Sounded like you said, 'Mom,'" he
said.*

I don't know why we go over the old hurts
Again and again in our minds, the false starts
And true beginnings
           of a world we call the past,
As if it could tell us who we are now,
Or were, or might have been . . .

                      Edward Hirsch

Old hurts again...

*I've always felt a connection to the past.
I believe this yearning for what was or
what never could be is a large part of
any creativity.*

*In recent years, from 1990 to the
present, I've begun in earnest a search
for family history and documented this
history in the paintings. For the first
time, pieces of the puzzle have fallen
into place and I've begun to feel whole.*

*Of all the relationships with my
family, the one between my mother
and me has been the most confusing.*

*My mother has always had her own
brand of excellence and good intentions,
which have made me uneasy for as long
as I can remember. It's taken a long
while to sort out misplaced childhood
priorities, the difference between celebrity and substance, and to find a way
out of the so-called American Dream.*

*My mother's generation taught me
I couldn't stay bound to its values—nor
could I depend on her for self-esteem.
With age and a little distance, I look
past all our old hurts and think of her
as the little girl who posed proudly
with her doll in the snow. As a woman,
I appreciate her strength of conviction
and try to get beyond the determined
force of one that she represented when
she stood behind my brother seeking
custody of my son.*

I know people hurt you—so bad
They don't know the damage they can do
and it makes me so sad . . .

Don Henley / Danny Kortchmar /
Ben Tench

As I began exploring our family history, I realized that when I was young my mother made tremendous efforts to shelter me from what she perceived as life's unpleasantries. She avoided disclosing details of her own childhood and I've concluded it wasn't a particularly happy one. She's always had the ability to dismiss what she doesn't want to see, and her coping skills were developed early. I benefited from every privilege she was ever denied; as a kid, I was very spoiled, but I suffered as an adult from her editing of life's sterner stuff.

I grew up believing I had a safety net attached—that there was always someone to catch me if I fell—in fact, give me crutches and do most of the walking for me.

When I stopped playing pretend, I was forty years old and on my own, supporting my four children for the first time—a frightening initiation into reality.

For all his accomplishments, my father rarely talked about himself, either. An athlete, All-American, winner of the Heisman trophy, he was a humble, uncomplicated, and deeply spiritual man. I didn't understand the depth of competitive spirit that lay within him until I was much older.

My childish interrogations into their lives led only to averted eyes and a change of subject. I got my parents' message. Theirs was a more guarded generation. Curiosity would have to wait.

*I wish
I'd been your confidante
there were so many things
we didn't talk about
I would have understood*

*we needed to put true feelings
into words
it would have been easier
for you and me*

*it was lonely
all these years*

*you insisted on a careful life
an orchestrated life
a happy happy life for me*

*I only needed
honesty
the truth*

*how were you to know
that by sparing me
the damage was done*

*emotional pain
wasn't your intention*

*It would have been nice
to share our feelings
instead of pretense and pretend*

*I would have understood
that generations of silence
can flow from a single choice
generation before generation
one generation after another*

I would have understood

203

THE VOICES REMAIN

1993

I would eventually complete the histories of my ancestors' lives and, contrary to my mother's fears, have great admiration for their courage and resourcefulness.

My hunt for information began by soliciting cousins, relatives, and friends for anything that might be informative. The generosity of their response was overwhelming. From attics and dusty trunks, from the United States and Europe, came wonderful old scrapbooks, correspondence, diaries, and photographs that helped to fill in the missing pieces.

I learned of the circumstances of my maternal grandmother's arrival at Ellis Island in the first decade of the twentieth century:

Her birth name was Hermina Sofia Mück. She was born in Vienna in 1896 and took the last name of Nagele when she was adopted by her aunt and uncle in 1909. Her friends called her Mina, but she was always Nana to me.

My grandmother's presence was my lifeline to reality. She had a mischievous sense of humor and a twinkle in her eye. She was comforting and courageous—the only person in the household whom my father didn't cross.

I miss her every day. She was so much a part of my life growing up, it never occurred to me that she wouldn't be around anymore.

Nana was two years old when her mother died. Her father remarried a woman who had little time for a child from another relationship. She went to work when she was very young, and her life in Austria was one of illness and hardship.

My grandmother made the long voyage in steerage from Hamburg to New York when she was thirteen, with her aunt and little cousin, Otto. She did not speak English when she arrived at Ellis Island in 1910.

With the help of my mother's recollections and letters from my aunt, I learned what I could about my maternal grandfather:

He was a handsome Austrian named Frederick Kornbrath who met my seventeen-year-old grandmother at a Sunday afternoon social outside of Hartford, Connecticut. During the early years of their marriage, he worked in one of the city's gun factories, played the zither, and sang beautifully, encouraging his children to sing along with him. But before too long he would become a tyrant to his family.

My grandfather hunted the wild animals that my mother loved. Mom remembers a man indifferent toward these animals, which horrified and saddened her and accounts for her enduring compassion toward all creatures. As a child, she was forbidden by her father to touch his hunting dogs or to have a pet of her own. To this day, she rescues and cares for strays of every variety. Growing up, we cohabited with many grateful pets.

"...those who live the secret wrong and badly (and they are very many), lose it only for themselves and still hand it on, like a sealed letter, without knowing it."

Rainer Maria Rilke

THE
GOOD SAMARITAN

1990

I never met my grandfather, but I have a strong memory of the day the call came in the living room on Sunswept Drive. I was still very young and it had been years since my grandfather had been a part of their lives. When my grandmother was informed of his death she handed the receiver to my mother, walked away, and said, "Good riddance," to no one in particular. I don't remember my mother saying anything at all.

My mother was born in Connecticut in 1917. She and her brother lived with my grandmother, who worked as a cook to support the family after my grandfather left. Mom made many of her clothes from her own designs, and her artistic talent was encouraged by her Uncle John, or R. J. Kornbrath, as he was known, who was a master engraver of prized firearms.

Uncle John—her father's brother—was my mother's favorite relative. As a child, Mom spent many hours in his studio—a small room on the fifth floor above the Bank of Hartford. She would sit quietly by the single worklight and watch him etch intricate designs freehand onto the guns of famous collectors.

I sometimes wonder if the detail in my paintings comes by way of Uncle John.

My mother passed on a love of the aesthetic to her children. When we were growing up, her purse always contained pen and paper (or rather the cardboard bottoms from the small packets of Kleenex) should we ever be inspired to draw.

After high school, she attended a school of design in New York City and planned on a career in fashion. She worked part-time as a photographer's assistant and was often asked to substitute for models who failed to report for work. Talent scouts discovered her on a fashion newsreel, and Twentieth Century-Fox studios in Hollywood asked her to screen-test.

In 1938, my mother and my grandmother took the train west. My mother was signed to a long-term contract by Fox.

Nana and Mom moved into their first real home—a little house with a red tiled roof in the Westwood section of Los Angeles. The following year—when Michigan came to California to play in a football game—my mother was introduced to my father when his team visited her movie set.

BABES
© Kristin Nelson Tinker
2-3-92

My mother never regretted giving up her life as an actress, but she refocused a great deal of her energy on mothering us. This created a complicated set of feelings in me—I wanted her to leave me alone with the same ferocity with which I demanded her attention.

The certificate of merit still hangs in my studio:

The students of my sixth-grade class at Marymount were asked to submit a poster for a national poster contest. I drew four animals on poster board—painted them in and lettered the theme SAVE THE ANIMALS *across the top.*

Mom asked to see the poster and her effusive compliments came pouring forth. I wanted her praise, but her encouraging words had the opposite effect. They didn't seem real, somehow. In my mind, I had a nagging feeling that anything I did on my own would somehow be taken as a diminishment of her.

As I recall—her reaction to the poster came with some suggestions for improvement, but I didn't take her advice. Placing it next to my bed for school the next day, I went to sleep.

When I awoke the next morning—my poster had changed drastically. It hardly resembled the childish drawing I'd done the night before. Sometime during the night my mother had "fixed" it. She peeked around the corner, smiling.

"Do you like it?" she asked.

I froze. I couldn't speak. No one would believe I did THAT.

It was now perfection—beautifully proportioned and shaded—magically transformed by the hand of someone who was an accomplished artist—not a ten-year-old. "Uh-huh," I said.

Mom's poster won a national award that year. I was the youngest student in my school to be presented with an honor in art. I accepted the certificate in a formal presentation at the eighth-grade graduation. It was— a BIG deal.

My mother and I never mentioned her contribution to my prize. I felt deceitful and guilt-ridden—the loneliest sixth-grader in the world—but I never felt bad enough to confess. Mom bragged about me to her friends, and the whole family was very proud. I didn't paint again for a long time.

SPECIAL
ANGELS

1992

On August 11, 1992, a new generation begun in our family. I was standing in the reception area of St. John's hospital in Santa Monica, California, where the sky outside was turning pink. It was expected to be one of the hottest days of the year. Tracy and Billy were due to check in any minute. It was the day my granddaughter was to be born.

When they arrived, Billy was holding Tracy's hand. In his other hand were pink-banded cigars. They had asked me to be with them for their daughter's birth.

Remington Elizabeth Moses came into the world at 3:12 PM. She was a combination of her mother and her father and of her grandparents, too. I wish my father were here today— I can see the look of pride as he holds his first great-grandchild.

Watching this little miracle take her first bath, I thought about Rick and how happy he would have been today—as proud and full of wonder as when his own children were born. An unexpected melancholy passed over me when I realized he'd never know his grand- children. How was it possible or fair? Wasn't it only yesterday that he was here with us? I remembered a story his father often told.

Rick was always a solitary little boy, a private person who dressed in combinations of cowboy, sports star, and action hero and tuned in to the classical music station on his parents' living room console. He would fall asleep in the corner of the big room as the music from the speaker surrounded him in sound and the air from the heating vent comforted his tiny body. He was, his father would say, a true lover of music.

Farewell! I did not know thy worth;
    But thou art gone, and now 'tis prized:
So angels walk'd unknown on earth,
    But when they flew were recognized.
                Thomas Hood

THE HEATER, THE CORNER,
AND THE MUSIC

1993

A sepia photograph came in the mail from my cousin in Rapid City—a picture of my paternal grandparents on their wedding day. They are posed formally—he's leaning slightly back—wearing a morning suit and high-collared shirt, his hair parted to one side, revealing a handsome face. My grandmother is seated in a wicker chair, wearing a dress of eyelet and Irish lace. Her eyes are slightly averted, but she sits straight and proud. I see my father in her.

My grandfather, Louis Anthony Harmon, was born in America. He was the fourth of seven children. His father came to America from Alsace-Lorraine, France. My grandmother's family were second-generation Irish-Americans originally from counties Tyrone and Donegal in Ireland.

I painted Harmons of the Heartland *from a description of my grandparents' wedding day found in a transcript of a speech given to honor their golden wedding anniversary on April 20, 1948, at the Hotel Gary in Gary, Indiana:*

"It is hard to think how many cakes were baked, and plentifully iced, how many loaves of bread stood rising in the pans, how many chickens had been taken out behind the woodhouse, or how many cans of homemade pickles had been brought from the cellar. There was a daylong party and the big Quinn house overflowed with young and old friends, even including the babies. The older generation chatted under the trees and ate as much as it was humanly possible until they one by one fell by the wayside and by evening the young folks were left free to roll back the rugs and dance."

HARMONS
OF THE HEARTLAND

1993

My father's mother visited us once in 1949, three years before she died. She had a habit of wearing a hairnet low on her forehead and bunching her words in staccato bursts that reminded me of the nuns at school. When I think of my grandmother Rose, I have a memory of the color green. I don't know if this was because she wore a green dress or because she gave me a green rosary or because she was Irish.

The Harmons were devout Catholics. My father, Thomas Dudley, was the youngest of seven children. He was born at home on September 28, 1919.

In 1925, the Harmons moved to Gary, Indiana, where the steel mills provided more job opportunities for my grandfather. Rose retired from teaching and took in boarders to help support the family. The Harmons were a lively group. From what I've gathered, there weren't many dull moments in the house on Jefferson Street.

I was still very young when my grandfather passed away, but I have my mother's memory of him as a kind and gentle man.

GRANDMA ROSE'S
ROSARY

1993

Years and years of nuns.

I liked the ceremony of being Catholic—the hand-made shrines with birthday candles and geraniums—veils for Benediction—the colored enamel of Saint Christopher medals. One particularly remembered homework assignment was to construct a miniature altar where scraps of gold material, from my Sugar Plum days, were incorporated into a tiny tabernacle.

Those were the good memories. But, overall, Catholicism terrified me— and caused conflict and confusion. The rules that were security for other Catholics only instilled high anxiety. Everywhere I went, another sin waited to happen. I was a sinner by virtue of living through the day and there was no getting around it. When I questioned, the nuns maintained that my sweet grandmother would burn in hell for eternity for not attending Mass on Sunday.

I was devastated. I worried about my father's frequent Friday night absences from the dinner table—suspecting that while I was relegated to eating fish sticks, he was out somewhere enjoying a nice prime rib.

I was afraid of the dark, of the end of the world, of going to sleep. Stories of the martyrs meant to inspire— caused nightmares involving gruesome amounts of blood.

Burning eternally wasn't something I looked forward to, but I couldn't seem to find an alternative.

We had to memorize pages of mortal and venial sins, but I never received clarification on what they meant. My fear was so great, I didn't ask for explanations.

Life was hard enough. Years later, when I could think it through, I decided I wouldn't be a part of a religion based on fear. I would find God in my own way.

I was always searching when I dreamed of Sunswept—as if I'd left something behind—something even dreams couldn't discern. Maybe I could find it going back —whatever it was.

In 1980, after seventeen years of marriage, I had to find a place to live. Coincidentally, I learned that my childhood home was for lease. I don't know why I thought that I could go back or that my problems would be solved by living there again. I couldn't afford the rent anyway, but curiosity overcame practicality and I returned for another look.

I remember the house on Sunswept Drive with delicious smells coming from Nana's kitchen—Bill Haley and the Comets on my portable 45—a poodle skirt hanging in the closet. Now, everything looked so small. The house was worn and used up and it smelled like dust. I wanted my mother to make it beautiful again—but she didn't live there anymore, either—she'd moved years ago with the rest of us. Where were the nooks and crannies of my childhood? What happened to my first private place—the storage space above the closet with the shoe-shelf ladder?

Why didn't I realize it was time to grow up?

It's impossible to conjure up images of Christmas without thinking of Sunswept Drive and my father. The two are inseparable.

About December 15th, my father would declare it time to begin his search for the perfect tree. My mother would pretend to bundle us up—the temperature was always around 65°, but we just knew it was cold enough to snow (those could be snow clouds, you know) and we would pile into the pink Oldsmobile station wagon for the short drive to the tree lots on Ventura Boulevard.

After an inspection of every Douglas fir and Colorado silver tip, a narrowing-down of his selection, and a conference with my mother, my father would pronounce his selection for that year—the fattest—most perfect—tree he'd ever seen.

He'd say, "Skip! Put 'er in the wagon!" (He called all young boys "Skip.") Then he'd whistle because he was happy.

Putting the lights on the tree was Dad's self-appointed job. Days could pass and many a fuse blown (we knew not to notice when this happened) before the lights were placed to his satisfaction.

Ornament hanging was women and kids' work. Dad would return to his favorite place in front of the television until it was time to supervise the fine art of tinsel hanging.

"Only one or two strands . . . be sure it hangs straight . . . not in the way of anything else . . . one or two strands . . . that's three or four . . . don't throw it . . ." Directions rivaling the Great Santini.

My father was sentimental and loved to shop for just the right gift. One year, he gave my mother lingerie of every description and color—all individually and personally wrapped. That year, it seemed like there were a hundred boxes under the tree.

Another Christmas
When my father'd had a good year
he placed
a solitary gift
for my mother
under the tree

The card with the red Santa read
"to Butch with love"
the box wasn't very big
hardly noticeable
his way
of a bigger surprise

My mother opened her gift
and found
to her astonishment
packed tightly in tissue

a full-length blonde mink coat

and my father
glowing
and grinning
from
ear to ear

ALL IS CALM, ALL IS BRIGHT
© KRISTIN NELSON TINKER
1992

In 1958, when I was in the eighth grade, our family moved from the heat and coziness of Sunswept Drive to a two-story house in Brentwood, where—it seemed—the sun never shined.

The house on North Carmelina Avenue was built by Greta Garbo in the thirties. We lived there until, one by one, the children moved out and my parents and grandmother bought a smaller and more comfortable house in the same neighborhood. Carmelina was a house to worry about because my parents worried—always in need of repair and my father complaining about the bills. The house was big and impersonal and it smelled like wet earth.

I rarely dream of Carmelina, but when I do, it comes with a Sunswept Christmas.

ALL IS CALM,
ALL IS BRIGHT

1992

"There is here no measuring with time, no year matters, and ten years are nothing. Being an artist means, not reckoning and counting, but ripening like the tree which does not force its sap and stands confident in the storms of spring without the fear that after them may come no summer. It does come. But it comes only to the patient, who are there as though eternity lay before them, so unconcernedly still and wide. I learn it daily, learn it with pain to which I am grateful: *patience* is everything!"

Rainer Maria Rilke

The dream begins in black and white. There is a house again.

It sits on top of a hill

and looks past a pool of water

to the different times of my life. I can see the ocean, boats, and birds.
My hands are young and capable—my eyesight is keen.
I am well within, and what I've left behind or what I am searching for is present here—in front of me.
This is the view I want to share.

There is music, *and flowers in my garden.*

I see my grandmother cooking in her kitchen in her house in the canyon across the way. She's with my mother,

who is carrying a basket of roses.

My grandmother is wearing a white gardenia.

My father is building a new house for them up the hill. My sister and her family are there.
In their houses, my children are singing.

My family and all the people I have loved

in my life are with me—inhabitants of this hill. Reggie, Rose, Max, Byron, and all my sweet pets are here with me, too.

I am peaceful, *and* content

and prolific *here. The gifts of my birth*

that were lost through my youth and stupidity and bullheadedness have returned to me.
From this perspective, I have confidence as a painter. I am a woman capable of insight, intimacy, and compassion.

I do not forget my brush strokes that are now light as air.

The dream melts to color.

June, 1996

The last months haven't been an easy time. I struggle with an imperfect ending to the dreams that are real within me. I'd anticipated a feeling of accomplishment when I finished this book, but instead found a sense of loss. I'd like to be able to write "she lived happily ever after," but it's not true. Life didn't happen that way.

The exterior life, this business of relationship and marriage, is raw stuff—unpredictable, lonely, intense, exquisite. The inner life, where clarity and possibility remain intact, is more peaceful for me—a much safer place.

So I look toward tomorrow with a spirit still hopeful —uneven amounts of courage and passion—the wisdom the years have brought—and a basket of brushes and paint.

SANTA MONICA
SEVEN

1990

Plate List

Permissions and Credits

I am grateful to the following people for giving me permission to use their correspondence, drawings, and words: John Boylan, Lisa Knox Burns, Elyse Knox Harmon, John Longenecker, Don Nelson, Gunnar Nelson, Matthew Nelson, Sam Nelson, Tracy Nelson, the Estate of Rick Nelson, Wally Franson, and Mark Tinker.

All unattributed poems are by Kristin Nelson Tinker.

CHAPTER FIVE

CHAPTER SIX